Coco Chanel

Titles in the series Critical Lives present the work of leading cultural figures of the modern period. Each book explores the life of the artist, writer, philosopher or architect in question and relates it to their major works.

Coco Chanel

Linda Simon

REAKTION BOOKS

Published by Reaktion Books Ltd
33 Great Sutton Street
London EC1V ODX, UK

www.reaktionbooks.co.uk

First published 2011

Printed and bound in Great Britain
by Bell & Bain, Glasgow

British Library Cataloguing in Publication Data
Simon, Linda, 1946–
    Coco Chanel. – (Critical lives)
    1. Chanel, Coco, 1883–1971.
    2. Women fashion designers – France – Biography.
    3. Fashion designers – France – Biography.
    I. Title II. Series
    746.9'2'092-dc22

ISBN 978 1 86189 859 3

Contents

Coco Chanel in a photograph by Boris Lipnitzki, 1936.

Introduction

Chanel appears as the living incarnation of her creations.
French *Vogue*, 1926

'In 1919', Coco Chanel said, 'I woke up famous.'[1] In fact, fame grew in the next few years as she created her first perfume, No. 5, in 1921 and her iconic little black dress in 1926. But in 1919 she was famous enough, cited in fashion magazines and newspapers, a rising star in a fashion world of many competitors. Jeanne Lanvin was famous too, as was Madeleine Vionnet; so were Jenny, Jean Patou, Madeleine Cheruit, Premet, Molyneux, Martial et Armand, Redfern, Renée, and of course the venerable Englishman Charles Frederick Worth. Around 40 couturiers were famous in 1919 and yet, nearly 100 years later, Chanel is the name that has survived, synonymous with high fashion: the *haute* of *haute couture*. Chanel has survived as a legend.

This is the triumph attributed to Chanel: she liberated women from corsets, bustles, floor-length dresses and beribboned, feathered hats; she urged women to move, in and out of cars for one thing, onto horses – if they chose – and into the workplace, just as she had done. She bobbed her hair and women followed; she introduced them to androgyny and they revelled in a new image; and she told them to wear soft, comfortable clothing such as men's sweaters (jauntily belted), men's shirts (open at the neck to reveal strands of fake pearls) and fabrics usually associated with menswear (like tweed and jersey). Chanel, so the legend goes, changed not only the shape of clothing but also the narrative of women's lives. She invented not only the simple black chemise, but also the modern woman.

To say that she was a fashion designer hardly captures her social and cultural significance. From 1913 onwards, when she first opened a hat shop in Deauville, until her death in 1971, Chanel sold more than clothing, accessories and a phenomenally successful perfume: she sold a myth that became as attractive for many women as her body-skimming dresses and bouclé suits. Her most flamboyant creation was her public persona: glamorous, slender, sexually independent, a playgirl who cavorted with the rich and famous. Alluring and charismatic, with a breathtaking genius for publicity and self-promotion, Chanel was the first celebrity couturière. Like any celebrity, her fame was based partly in reality – the reality of her artistry and vision – and partly in desire: her own relentless desire for adulation, as well as her public's, for a bold image of feminine power and sexuality. For generations of women, Chanel embodied possibility, achievement and – most of all – defiance.

This book teases apart the myth that Chanel and her public collaborated to create, explores its contradictions, and examines the world that she both reflected and shaped. Chanel flourished in – and contributed to – a culture of notoriety that enabled her to achieve startling success, and she helped to change the dissemination of fashion that made the Chanel name and brand known far beyond the rarefied world of *haute couture*.

Certainly, she was an iconoclastic entrepreneur who rebelled against and manipulated the gender expectations of her time, but she also championed deeply held cultural assumptions about women's roles and their relationships to men. Certainly, her designs were beautiful and coveted, and often they astutely and elegantly responded to popular fashion trends. Certainly, Chanel had taste and flair. She boasted a refined sense of smell and many who witnessed her success argue that she had as refined a presentiment of women's unspoken needs. She herself, deeply superstitious, attributed a certain amount of her success to luck: being in the right place, in the right business, at exactly the right time. 'My time was ready for me, waiting', she said, 'all I had to do was come on the scene.'[2] But luck does not explain the enduring myth of Coco Chanel.

In 1913, when Chanel was a milliner selling boater hats that she bought at the Galeries Lafayette and decorated with streamers and ribbons, fashion magazines already showed a new silhouette: slim, with fluid lines, in soft fabrics. These magazines addressed active women who took up tennis, golf, yachting, horseback riding, camping and skiing. They danced energetically, and each issue of the upscale women's magazine *Femina* featured instructions for new dances – the turkey trot, '*le pas du double boston*', the one-step and the tango. 'Our epoch will be the epoch of energy, of health, and of balance', an editorial exclaimed.

In 1919, the year Chanel awoke to fame, drawings of designs by her competitors which were appearing in French fashion magazines all featured the same look as her own: trim and narrow. Fashion plates by illustrators such as Georges Lepape and Georges Barbier depicted slender young women with impossibly long legs and cropped hair, wearing low-waisted dresses in muted tones like grey and beige, and in fluid fabrics like silk or wool jersey. 'The sensational novelty of the season almost everywhere', reported *Vogue*, 'is the effect of a man's shirt or a shirt-front with a collar, and this collar is of infinite variety'.[3] But those other designers who helped to create the *garçonne* look did not embody the new woman as Chanel did; she not only designed for her generation, she wore her own designs everywhere and the outfits looked stunning on her.

She did not liberate women from the constriction of corsets – that credit goes to Paul Poiret and Madeleine Vionnet who had long before rejected the hourglass figure by designing soft, flowing,

Costume tailleur en cheviotte grise. Chemisette de Baptiste. Chapeau en paille
de riz garni velours noir et Guêtres de Drap beige.

Fashion plate
from *Journal
des dames et
des modes*
(1912), suit.

drapey dresses. But while they created costumes for women to
pose in, Chanel created outfits to live in, clothing that seemed to
caress a body that was – ideally – svelte and sexy. 'I will tell you a
secret', Chanel once confessed to an interviewer. 'I always try the
first models on myself in the studio. That way, I get the right proportions and feel the fit, the ease, the weight of the dress myself.'[4]
The right proportions for Chanel, though, were proportions that
few women could emulate but that many aspired to possess. With

Fashion plate from *Journal des dames et des modes* (1912), golfing outfit.

Blouse à plis creux en toile Kaki guêtres hautes en drap beige chapeau à feutre

the body of an adolescent boy, flat-chested and petite, Chanel kept herself bone thin. She admitted to weighing between 47 and 48 kg (103½ and 106 lb), slight even for someone a few inches over five feet (1.5 m). Many who dined at her table recalled that she hardly ate; one lamb chop and two lettuce leaves, a guest noted, was enough to suffice for dinner. She did not nourish herself, as another dinner companion put it, and she abhorred fat people. A good figure, she said, was more important than a pretty face.

Coco and Marthe
Davelli on a yacht
in 1930.

Chanel modelled a body image that could be achieved only through rigorous dieting and undergarments that flattened and bound the breasts and any other body parts that might interrupt an outfit's line. 'I hate breasts that show', she remarked. Women 'can have hips, that's all right, but in the front and the back, they should be flat like men'.[5] Fashion magazines ran articles about dieting, corset manufacturers found new ways to tame the body, cosmetic surgeons found new clients. Chanel's designs suggested to women an image of perpetual youth – an identity as eternal *ingénues* – and they longed to fulfil that identity.

If some customers interpreted her outfits as cross-dressing, as resistance against old-fashioned notions of femininity, or as any kind of protest at all, many more coveted Chanel's styles because they were sexy and seductive. 'Matrons depended on Vionnet, debutantes on Lanvin and sportswomen on Schiaparelli', *The Washington Post* proclaimed in 1936. 'But it is said that if a woman was trying to catch a man or hold her husband she invariably called on Chanel.'[6]

For much of her career, Chanel nurtured her reputation as successful entrepreneur who would not trade that success to become someone's wife, even if the suitor were, say, the Duke of Westminster. She was a flirt, a coquette and her affairs made the news. Items in the press linking her with one man and then another made her seem sexually liberated and independent, discarding lovers when they became tiresome or demanding. In her later years, though, she was forthright about revealing her loneliness and vulnerability. These revelations, rather than tarnish her legend, enhanced it, reflecting widespread ambiguity among women about the consequences of transgressing gender boundaries and risking loss of their own femininity. 'Freedom and independence are not the same', Chanel explained. 'Pity the woman *en liberté*. She has no one and is dependent on everyone. Independence is something else. Of course, if she achieves it, it means unhappiness.'[7] Several times she believed she was close to marrying, but each time she lost her lover, usually because he married someone else: richer, younger, fertile or a member of the aristocracy. When she was 50 years old, the man she hoped to marry dropped dead on a tennis court before her eyes, the victim of a heart attack. Thirty years later, she died alone, bitter, raging against old age and against a world (including the world of fashion) to which she felt little connection. 'Solitude may help a man towards achievement', she admitted, 'but it destroys a woman.'[8]

Her 'maxims' – often appearing in fashion magazines and repeated in her interviews – reveal ideas about love and sex closer to the nineteenth century than the legendary wild 1920s or turbulent '60s, ideas that were likely also held by those who looked up to her: by Marilyn Monroe, for example, who famously responded when asked what she wore to bed: nothing but Chanel No. 5. 'A woman', Chanel pronounced, 'is a force not properly directed. A man is properly directed. He can find refuge in his work. But work just wipes a woman out. The function of a woman is to be loved.' Or: 'Women ought to play their weakness, never their strength. They ought to hide that.' Or: 'A woman who's not loved is no woman. Whatever her age. A woman who's not loved is a woman who's lost. The only thing for her to do is die.'[9] This is the advice that Chanel, wealthy and powerful as she was, shared with her contemporaries.

Yet despite her desire to be cherished and protected, Chanel ran her couture house aggressively, intimidating workers, fashion editors and even some customers. Although she had learned to sew as a young girl, Chanel did not sew as a designer and she could not draw. She excelled at ripping and cutting. Scissors were her weapon and she wielded them with defiance, and sometimes rage. Her relationships with her workers were often volatile and frustrating. Models were forced to stand for an entire day as Chanel ripped apart an outfit that had been laboriously sewn

Marilyn Monroe photographed by Ed Feingersh, 1955. Monroe was a great fan of Chanel No. 5 and can be seen here holding the iconic perfume.

by her seamstresses, according to her own instructions. She was never satisfied with the first, or second, or even the tenth rendering of her wishes. Models walked and turned, and walked again. They raised their arms as Chanel evaluated the way a sleeve attached to a seam. Her mouth full of pins, she muttered abuses, reducing her assistants to tears. The workplace on the rue Cambon was thick with tension; but in the end, Chanel achieved the perfection that she desired.

Her social relationships could be equally volatile. As a young woman her impetuousness and dazzling smile served her well, and she seemed never without an admirer. She moved easily in the social circle of the famous and wealthy. But she was always afraid: of losing what she was not sure she deserved and of being exposed for who she really was. Throughout her life, Chanel perpetuated lies about herself to hide a past that she was ashamed to reveal and to insist upon a past that she considered suitable for an internationally famous designer. To keep herself safe she held people at a distance, pushing away anyone who might discover the truth. She lied to friends, she lied to would-be biographers, she lied so inventively and consistently that even today – decades after her death in 1971 – it's hard to get at the facts. Still, many writers have attempted to do so and this book relies on the investigations of biographers and memoirists who knew Chanel, as well as those who have been drawn to her as a subject during her lifetime and since her death, and on primary material in newspapers, magazines and archives.

These sources reveal a woman beset and sometimes undone by her own complexities: a champion of women who herself longed desperately for the protection of a man; a self-proclaimed recluse who emerged as one of the most spectacular personalities of her time; a brilliant businesswoman who signed away 90 per cent of her company; a world-renowned success who died sad and embittered; a genius who claimed she was nothing more than an artisan. 'Coco

Chanel', fashion historian Valerie Steele wrote, 'is probably the most important fashion designer of the twentieth century . . . Chanel was the woman that other women wanted to look like.'[10] Chanel was the woman that other women, for many decades, wanted to be.

1

A Small Dark Girl

You see if I told the truth, people would think I was dreadful,
even if I spoke badly of no one but myself.
Chanel[1]

'The child that I was is with me today', Chanel told Louise de
Vilmorin in the 1940s when Vilmorin had agreed to work with
her on her memoirs.[2] That statement is true, but the reality of her
childhood generated the lies that she embellished throughout her
life. Here is the story she told, as repeated by *Vogue* fashion editor
Bettina Ballard: Her mother died when she was a young child and
her father, her loving father, left for America in hopes of making
his fortune. She was brought up by two stern and elderly aunts on
a farm in the Auvergne, always waiting for her father to return as
he had promised. 'The aunts' stone house had small windows that
were always kept closed', she told Ballard, 'and they sat primly in
their rusty black dresses in the dark parlor sewing or reading, their
eyes on the small dark girl who was supposed to be studying or
sewing but who kept looking out of the windows'. The aunts
raised horses, and whenever the young Coco was able to escape
she threw herself on a horse and rode through the wild country-
side. Finally, when she was sixteen, she visited her grandfather at
Vichy; determined never to go back to her aunts' house, she stopped
a handsome young officer and asked him to take her away. The
officer was the wealthy Étienne Balsan.[3]

The reality was far different. Instead of being raised in bourgeois decorum, she was born into poverty, which to her would always mean vulgarity. Her father, Henri-Albert Chanel, was a travelling salesman and philanderer. When his second daughter Gabrielle (Coco) was born on 19 August 1883, he and Jeanne Devolle (Coco's mother) were living with their one-year-old daughter, Julia-Berthe, in a garret in Saumur in the department of Maine-et-Loire, 322 km (200 miles) west of Paris. By the time they married in November 1884, Jeanne was pregnant again. Marriage did nothing for Albert's reliability. Hoping to entice Albert to settle down, Jeanne often followed him when he went on the road, accompanied by their two daughters. But Jeanne's wishes for security were repeatedly dashed and only resulted in more pregnancies. By the time Gabrielle was eleven, Jeanne had given birth to four more children: Alphonse, Antoinette, Lucien and Augustin, who died in infancy. Albert witnessed neither his last son's birth nor his death. Instead, he often disappeared for long periods, leaving Jeanne as sole caretaker for their growing and impoverished family. Exhausted by pregnancies, Jeanne succumbed to severe asthma in 1895. Chanel transformed her mother's illness into tuberculosis, claiming to remember blood-stained handkerchiefs; she told of the horror of listening to her mother struggling for breath and dying in the next room – a scene that may, or may not, be true.

Chanel rarely spoke about her siblings' relationships to one another. Although she claimed that Antoinette, who was four years younger, was her favourite sister, there's no evidence from their childhood to suggest the quality of their relationship. As adults, Antoinette usually bowed to Chanel's will, devotedly helping her, a behaviour pattern that may have begun in their youth. Chanel had little interest in Julia, who was only one year older than she was, and showed more affection for her brother Alphonse with whom she could climb trees: Chanel portrayed herself as something of a tomboy.

Family life, whatever it had been for the children, ended in 1895. After Jeanne's death, there was no question about Albert taking care of his offspring. By the time she was twelve, Gabrielle and her sisters were living in a Catholic orphanage in Aubazine, while the boys were taken in by farm families. Later, Chanel insisted that a staircase in her villa in the south of France exactly reproduced the staircase at Aubazine: perhaps it was a form of homage, reminding her of how far she had come. In her early designs of black suits with wide white colours, some believe she evoked the nuns' habits that she remembered vividly. It was the nuns, after all, who taught her to sew and instilled in her a fetish for cleanliness that she would forever equate with virtue. One of the worst rebukes she made about someone was that he was dirty. One of the highest compliments was that a woman hid her 'personal odor' with a 'bit of "smell-good" . . . a well-perfumed woman is very agreeable', she thought.[4]

Chanel was an illegitimate child, an impoverished child, a child who was raised by the sisters of the Congregation of the Sacred Heart of Mary: those were the facts that Chanel wanted to obliterate from her life. Even the moment of her birth saddened her: she was born at dusk, she told people, and forever that time of day made her feel troubled and anxious. 'When I was a child, I wanted love. I didn't get it', she said. 'I used to set traps for it . . . I had a horrible childhood.'[5] She longed for her father. It was he, she said, who named her Coco. He had been away at the time of her birth and hated the name her mother had given her. He told her she should answer only to Coco. In another version, Chanel said that she was born in a hospital where Gabrielle Bonheur – 'Gabrielle Happiness' – happened to be the name of the nun who attended her mother for the delivery, and so the name was chosen by the hospital, not her mother.

She claimed to have been a solitary child who retreated into her imagination. She made necklaces out of flowers or autumn leaves, portending the creativity that would come later. She read novels (in secret) and these inspired her reveries and dreams. She told Claude Delay – an intimate friend during the last decade of her life – that the Brontë sisters were among her favourites: she had read both *Jane Eyre* and *Wuthering Heights*, which appeared in French translations within a few years of publication in England. In these novels, obstacles are overcome; suffering is rewarded; the heroine – the orphaned Jane Eyre, for example – finds true love. She also read popular romances serialized in local newspapers, fairy tales that enticed the young woman longing to be carried off by a handsome prince. 'The lies of novels', she said later. 'I had read so many of them. If I had children, I would raise them on novels. Everything is in them . . . Time gives us the rest.'[6]

She said everyone in her aunts' house (where she insisted she was raised) always talked about money. She overheard maids confiding to one another that as soon as they had saved enough money they would leave their menial employment. Money for her became synonymous with freedom. 'Very young', she said, 'I had realised that without money you are nothing, that with money you can do anything. Or else, you had to depend on a husband.'[7] She was twelve when she learned this essential truth – if not from her relatives, then from the orphanage, which taught her daily about her own poverty and powerlessness. Money would surely buy freedom, but also – the convent taught her – deliverance could occur through miracles and magic. Later, she would surround herself with charms. She had a lucky number, five, which was the date she set for all of her fashion show openings, and the number of her first perfume. She was relentlessly superstitious. 'You see this ring?' she asked an interviewer in 1957 when she came to America to accept a fashion award,

> I would trade all my other jewels for this. It was given to me when I was sixteen, in my home province of Auvergne, by an

old woman who liked me. She handed me the ring and said, 'Here, *petit Coco* . . . wear this ring always. Never, never let it leave your finger. It will bring you luck, your life will be magnificent.' What she said then, so long ago, has proved true – my life is magnificent.[8]

Where the ring really came from is less important than what Chanel wanted her public to believe.

She claimed that she never had an appetite in her aunts' house. Nothing tempted her. 'I was naughty, bad-tempered, thieving, hypocritical and eavesdropping', she told her friend Paul Morand, 'I only liked to eat what I had stolen.' She told him she cut thick slices of bread and ate them in the bathroom.[9] She was exhausted, filled with despair, disoriented. She longed for her father, telling herself that he loved her and had not wanted to leave her. She said that for her first communion her father had sent her a white dress from America, a dress so gaudy that her aunts thought it was chosen by a prostitute. But Gabrielle was enchanted by it: the dress meant that her father cared for her. 'In all the thousands of dresses that were to come', Claude Delay suggested, 'she would clothe women in her own emotion, endeavouring to make them less likely to be deserted, never resigning herself to that primal desertion'.[10] If there is one fact about her childhood that *can* be believed, it is that the young Gabrielle was convinced that her father would return to love her, to build her a beautiful house and to save her.

The young woman she portrayed in her depiction of her past is depressed, lonely, starving. 'Every day I thought about how to kill myself', she later told Delay.[11] 'The only beautiful eyes are those that look at you tenderly', became one of her repeated 'maxims'. She gave two versions of her reaction to her father's absence: in the first, she is so hungry for love that she is ready to give her heart to anyone who showed a bit of tenderness, in the second, she became strong and resolute in the face of what she decided was nothing less than abandonment. Abandonment is what she feared in every relationship, throughout her life.[12]

Chanel remained at Aubazine until she was eighteen, and then became a charity student at a boarding school run by the Sisters of Notre Dame in Moulins. Her aunt Adrienne – her grandparents' last child, who was only a year older than Chanel – was a student there, and Julia and Antoinette joined them. Still, even with three girls from her own family as company, Chanel was lonely. Paying students came from wealthy families and Chanel felt the difference daily.

Although Chanel sometimes left the school to visit her grandfather who was being treated at a spa in Vichy, her rescue did not come from any officer she met there. Instead, she spent a year and a half as a seamstress and salesgirl in a lingerie shop in the garrison town of Moulins, working alongside Adrienne, making a bit of extra money on the side by working for a local tailor. Customers included wives of officers quartered in the town, wealthy women who resided in the region's chateaux or who came for the racing season and, at the tailor's shop, the officers themselves. At first, both young women shared an attic room in a house owned by their employers, but by the time she was twenty-one Chanel decided to find a room that would afford her more independence, and Adrienne soon joined her. The two, taken to be sisters, began to attract the attention of men.

It was on one of her dates that Chanel went to La Rotonde, a cabaret that featured singers every evening. Amateurs were invited to try out for a gig and Chanel took up the invitation. Although her voice was small, something about her flirtatious manner won the director's admiration. Among the few songs she knew, one was 'Qui qu'a vu Coco?' about a Parisian searching for her lost dog, and the other was 'Ko ko ri ko', the title song of a recent Paris variety show. From the time of her Moulins entertaining career, Gabrielle became Coco. And Coco became the lover of Étienne Balsan.

Balsan was 24 years of age, the youngest son of successful textile manufacturers. His parents were dead; his two older brothers had taken over the family business, but Étienne wanted none of it. He wanted to raise and ride horses, and when his tour with the cavalry had finished he bought an estate at Royallieu, once owned by a racetrack trainer. When he suggested that Chanel accompany him there to see the horses, she agreed immediately.

There is no reason to doubt that – as Chanel later claimed – Balsan was her lover, even her first lover. He may have got her pregnant. She may have undergone an abortion that left her infertile. Or maybe not. She may have loved him and thought that he loved her. She may have believed that he would send away his mistress, the actress Émilienne d'Alençon, whom he had already ensconced on the estate. She may even have believed that he would marry her. Among the stories she told about her liaison with Balsan was that his brothers, embarrassed by his dalliances with women like d'Alençon, had pressed Coco to marry him. But she refused; she didn't love him, she claimed.

What *is* certain is that she lived with Balsan at Royallieu for six years, beginning when she was 22. With Balsan she got to socialize with people far richer than any she had ever known, and they intimidated her. If she seemed fearless on a horse and amusing in the grandstands, her behaviour concealed deep anxiety. 'I was a little girl scared of everything', she told Marcel Haedrich, a rare confidant. 'A little girl who knew nothing, absolutely nothing about anything.'[13] It is possible that she was brought out in public but kept sequestered in private, eating apart from the main dining hall where Balsan entertained his friends.

At Royallieu, Chanel first began to wear jodhpurs, shirt sleeves, unadorned felt hats and ties. The outfits – with the exception of the jodhpurs – were not essentially different from what other sporting women wore: long riding jackets over white shirts. But while other women wore long, heavy skirts, Chanel had jodhpurs

Chanel, 1909.

sewn specifically for her. When evening entertainment included mounting amateur theatricals, Chanel often dressed as a man or an adolescent boy. In the morning, she might have wrapped herself in Balsan's oversized bathrobe. These outfits only served to make her look more girlish, and certainly to distinguish her from someone like Émilienne with her corsets, laces, flounces and frills. Even when Chanel wore women's outfits, these were tailored conservatively, often a bit too long and too loose. The effect was to make Chanel herself seem even smaller, slighter and more delicate than she was: demure and in need of protection.

Chanel in a wide-brimmed hat, 1910.

Among the many men she met at Royallieu, one interested her more than all the rest: the Englishman Arthur Capel, called 'Boy'. A year older than Chanel, Capel was already a wealthy businessman whose family had made a fortune from coal mines. If his fortune was not as hefty as Balsan's, it hardly mattered. With residences in London and Paris, and with a stable of horses, he seemed far more cosmopolitan, worldly and well-educated than Balsan, and far more attractive. He was, Chanel told Paul Morand, 'a rare spirit, an unusual character; a young man who had the experience of a fifty-year old, a gentle, playful authority; and an ironic severity that charmed people and won them over'. Where Balsan treated Chanel as a frivolity, a plaything, Capel – she believed – saw her as a woman with potential, a woman who wanted to be moulded; she would allow him to serve as her Pygmalion because she respected him for his 'deep inner life that extended to magical and theosophical levels'.[14] It is likely that she believed that Capel, like Pygmalion, would marry his Galatea. Claiming later that he was the only man she ever loved, Chanel added: 'He shaped me, he knew how to develop what was unique in me, at the cost of everything else.'[15] Although Chanel said that they did not appear in public together, others recall that they first met Chanel in Capel's company, either in Deauville or in Italy.

According to Claude Delay, Chanel said that intercourse had been so painful for her that Capel brought her to see a physician friend of his. He 'sensed the trouble' and assured her that he could help. 'A snip of the scissors cleared the threshold of her life as a woman', Delay wrote.[16] Chanel's enormous relief at the success of the procedure suggests that her previous sexual relations, with Balsan and perhaps others, had caused her great physical distress. Yet it was through sex that Chanel saw a way to the world she desired.

Hoping to marry Capel, she still wanted to earn money in her own right. There were two reasons she wanted to work: first, she said she was bored. But boredom – which she hated and feared – was not the only reason; she hated and feared financial indebtedness as well. For Chanel, independence meant self-sufficiency. 'To begin with, you long for money', she said. 'Then you develop a liking for work. Work has a much stronger flavour than money. Ultimately, money is nothing more than the symbol of independence. In my case, it only interested me because it flattered my pride.'[17]

Several people who worked with her claimed that designing was not an inevitable career for Chanel, but one in which she thought she would be successful. By the time she neared 30, the only jobs she had ever had were sewing and cabaret singing. As she was deciding the next step in her career, she undertook a brief effort as a student of eurhythmic dance, popularized then by Isadora Duncan.

Chanel's teacher was the flamboyant cancan dancer and choreographer Caryathis. Her experience with Caryathis, though, convinced her that the stage was not her destiny; still, her interest in becoming an entertainer raises a question about the contradiction between her self-confessed shyness and her penchant for exhibitionism. Once she opened her own shop, she claimed that she hid from customers out of fear of interacting with them; later in her life, she explained that she talked compulsively to hide her social awkwardness. Yet she seemed ready, in 1912, to take centre stage as a performer. Soon, however, she realized that her talents lay more with fabrics and thread than in a nightclub. She had earned praise for the hats she had made, or redesigned, for society women who visited at Royallieu. Their delight led her to believe that she could make a living as a milliner.

When Chanel confessed her aspirations to Balsan and Capel, they offered measured encouragement. Why not do something to keep busy, they thought, even if becoming a milliner would not make her rich? Balsan, who was on his way to Argentina's horse country for what he planned as a long stay, agreed to lend her his ground-floor Paris apartment on Boulevard Malesherbes to use as a shop. Capel, who lived nearby on Avenue Gabriel, gave the project his blessings and financial backing. For Chanel, his encouragement translated as evidence of his love and she luxuriated in his attentions. Within a year she moved into Capel's apartment, while keeping her shop in Balsan's.

Curious clients visited; some made purchases and many brought friends. Chanel's repertoire of designs, however, was not enough to sustain a growing business. She bought plain hats from Galeries Lafayette and trimmed them in her jaunty way. But her clientele demanded more. On Capel's recommendation Chanel hired a prominent milliner, Lucienne Rabaté (then working at the Maison Lewis boutique), who brought with her two able assistants. To staff the shop, she hired her younger sister Antoinette.

Fashion plate from *Journal des dames et des modes* (1913), riding outfit.

1913   Costumes Parisiens   126

Une Amazone

With Rabaté bringing considerable expertise and ideas to the boutique, Chanel expanded her offerings and attracted more customers – including mistresses of wealthy men, actresses and members of the aristocracy. Needing more space both for work-rooms and sales, Chanel pleaded for a larger venue. Capel helped her to find space on the fashionable rue Cambon, no. 21, near the Hotel Ritz and Place Vendôme. Chanel took his gesture as affirmation of her business success but actually she was earning little.

Her difficulties with employees began immediately. While Antoinette was hard-working and docile, Lucienne Rabaté had her own strong ideas – both about designs and Chanel's relationships with customers – but Chanel resented her suggestions. When Rabaté advised Chanel to avoid making appointments for one man's wife and mistress at the same time, Chanel refused to listen. When Rabaté advised Chanel to turn away a notorious 'actress' so as not to offend a host of wealthy women customers, Chanel refused to listen. Finally, Rabaté decided to leave.

In a scene that would repeat itself throughout her career, Chanel managed to charm Rabaté and convince her to return . . . at least for a while. With Rabaté once again designing, Chanel set out to attract new customers by publicizing her style. With Capel she now and then visited Royallieu and the resort town of Deauville. Wherever she went, she was noticed, not only for the distinctive hats that she wore but for some striking, apparently careless, fashion choices. She might appear walking in town wrapped in one of Capel's polo sweaters, for example, or on the beach wearing a sailor's shirt open at the neck. But besides flaunting these outfits, she began, simply, to be seen in places where artists, writers and musicians were seen, entering a world supported by – but not limited to – the wealthy aristocracy. Chanel's ability to merge these two worlds was decisive in her rise to fame.

According to Chanel's biographers Edmonde Charles-Roux and Axel Madsen, a significant moment in her entry into the world of art and music occurred on Thursday, 29 May 1913. On this unusually sultry evening, these writers assert, Chanel accompanied her friend and former teacher Caryathis to the newly completed Théâtre des Champs-Elysées. A sleek concrete and marble structure designed by the modernist architect Auguste Perret, the theatre proved an appropriate setting for an eagerly anticipated performance: the premiere of Sergei Diaghilev's Ballets Russes performing Igor Stravinsky's *Le Sacre du Printemps,* choreographed by Vaslav Nijinsky. Diaghilev chose the date because it was the first anniversary of the successful premiere of Nijinsky's *L'Après-midi d'un faune*, but even the auspicious date did not calm his nerves, nor those of the composer who was sitting in the fourth row. Nijinsky, his sister Romola and Diaghilev paced in the wings. The evening began with the romantic *Les Sylphides*, seemingly perfect for a spring night. But for weeks Diaghilev had circulated rumours that he was presenting something new, something provocative, and the subscription-only audience edgily awaited the second piece.

As Jean Cocteau later recalled, the theatre held 'all the raw materials for a scandal . . . a fashionable public, lapped in pearls, aigrets and ostrich plumes; and side by side with these tail coats and tulles, the business suits and bright bandeaux of that race of aesthetes which acclaims the new for no better reason than its hatred of the boxes'.[18] In other words, this cross-section of Parisian culture was hoping to be astonished and prepared to be outraged.

Their expectations were more than fulfilled: the orchestra had hardly begun and the curtain just lifted, when a battle erupted between those in the audience noisily offended by the strident chords and pounding dance, and those just as noisily exultant. Violent, primal, dissonant, the performance was like nothing this Parisian audience had ever experienced. 'People laughed, shrieked insults, hissed, imitated the cries of animals', and even began to insult and push one another, Cocteau remembered.[19] Women in diamond tiaras and silk couture gowns appeared to be whipped into madness.

Was Chanel among them? In later years, she told some she had attended but told her friend Paul Morand that she had not seen *Le Sacre du Printemps* before 1914. 'Serge spoke about it as if it had caused a scandal and had been a great historical moment', she said. And so in 1920 she gave Diaghilev a private gift to finance a revival of the ballet. How much did she give? 200,000 francs? 300,000? Whatever the amount – worth about £15,500 at the time – Diaghilev said it was 'a cheque exceeding his wildest hopes'.[20] She asked him to keep the gift secret, which he did not. Did she give him the gift because she wanted, at last, to see the performance? Because, as she said, she admired 'his zest for life, his passions, his scruffiness'?[21] Because she wanted Diaghilev to see her as more generous than their mutual friend Misia Sert? Or because, by then, she was having an affair with Stravinsky? Whatever the real reason, by 1921 Chanel was wealthy: more wealthy than she had ever dreamed.

2

Boaters

To please is to be someone who listens, who seems somewhat fragile.
Chanel, 1937[1]

Like many coastal towns in Normandy and Brittany, Trouville and
Deauville – separated by the narrow River Touques – were popular
summer destinations for Parisians and wealthy international tourists
seeking a luxurious respite from urban heat. Rivalry had long sim-
mered between the two cities, where for much of the nineteenth
century gambling and strolling along the beach formed the main
attractions. Trouville, which had villas dotting the hills rising from
the coast, barely won out, until 1862 when the enterprising Duc de
Morny (illegitimate half-brother of Louis-Napoléon Bonaparte) took
the initiative of building a racetrack in Deauville. Suddenly – especially in August and during the Grande Semaine that featured the
Grand Prix – Deauville became undeniably glamorous. A building
boom followed with hundreds of villas constructed along wide
avenues. A glittering new casino opened in 1912 and effusive press
coverage touted Deauville as the place to be and to be seen. As if
to underscore the sylvan setting, a quaint custom began which
had duchesses and countesses walking to market on Wednesdays
and Saturdays, baskets on their arms, buying their own fruits and
vegetables. Still, opulence was on display; the duchesses wore their
diamonds, even in the morning. Cornelius Vanderbilt's *North Star* and
Anthony Drexel's *Sayanara* were among the yachts docked at the pier.

By 1913, Deauville was, for Americans, the French Newport. For Europeans, it was the summer equivalent of Monte Carlo. The only reason to go to Trouville was if the Deauville hotels had no available rooms left. 'As soon as the Paris season ends, Deauville takes up its round of high life', reported the *New York Times*. Americans did not bother going to Paris at all but headed straight to Deauville, dubbed the 21st arrondissement. 'There, by paying five times as high as in the capital, they are able to live in miniature Paris by the sea among a crowd.'[2] Deauville was chic, cosmopolitan and very, very rich. 'Deauville Sands Blaze With Jewels', announced a headline in the *New York Times* just after the Grande Semaine ended in 1913.[3] If the Grand Prix punctuated the week's festivities, it was not the only occasion for the wealthy to flaunt their assets: the baccarat tables saw huge sums change hands, and invitations to luncheons, dinners and balls flew among the gathered elite.

Shopping, of course, was a favourite pastime – even if baccarat or the races did not yield winnings. The affluent Belmont, Biddle and Kellogg families, and a host of princes, marquises, countesses and duchesses, frequented the short street of shops in the centre of town where many famous Paris couturiers had established branches. There, on the Rue Gontaut-Biron (near the posh Hotel Normandie), the 30-year-old Chanel opened her own hat boutique, once again financed by Capel.

Her boutique was popular, as were most shops in the small centre. Photographs show dozens of men and women congregated around the doors, and the women's clothing reflects the fashion moment from which Chanel emerged. Older women were corseted with ample bosoms protruding above small waists, balanced by large-brimmed, feathered hats. Younger women, though, were often dressed in the slimmer styles that many designers had featured a few years earlier: long, looser jackets, boaters trimmed with simple ribbons, muted colours. The influence of men's fashions on women's styles had begun in the last quarter of the nineteenth century, when many young women showed a decided predilection for men's styles in jackets (some similar to riding coats) which they often wore with ties. The tailored suit – usually made by tailors rather than dress-makers – became popular in England, France and America among all ranks of women, from wealthy socialites to the working class. Rejecting heavily embellished hats, these women favoured straw boaters or added derby and fedora hats – and even jockey caps – to their wardrobe. Long, heavy skirts, leg-of-mutton sleeves and small defined waists, common in the 1890s, softened and loosened after the turn of the century.

In the autumn of 1912, even before Chanel's boutique opened, fashion reporters noted the popularity of the 'slim, slight silhouette'. Coats looked like a style a man might wear: straight and shapeless with a loose belt across the back. An American woman who tried it 'looked like a healthy boy', while a young French woman 'looked like a coquettish actress dressed up in a boy's costume'.[4]

The idea of youthfulness generated as much concern as did androgyny. In the year when Chanel opened her boutique, a *New York Times* fashion reporter noted with some anxiety the distinction between fashions for the young and slender and fashions for older, larger women. 'I have not seen a single gown at any opening yet that is designed for the American woman of 40 years old who has the height, the breadth, and the stateliness of her generation. What is she going to do?'[5] The current fashions of 1912 – from all the couturiers – were designed for thin, petite, young women who redefined femininity as a kind of adolescent insouciance.

Besides adopting the tubular line of dresses and suits, women affected a new way of walking: a listless slouch.

'The graceful feminine manners taught in the finishing schools seem to be quite out of date', reported the *New York Times*. 'The smart woman of the 1913 Winter season will not walk, but will slouch along with both hands in the pockets especially provided

Chanel in front of her boutique in Deauville, 'Boy' Capel is assumed to be sitting on her left.

A view from the street in Deauville in 1913 with women outside Chanel's boutique.

among the numerous full pleats of her skirt front, her shoulders pushed forward and the weight of the body resting entirely on the hips. This distorted appearance is the result, it is said, of the abolition of the corset and the adoption of extraordinarily wide and full clothes.'[6]

Although Chanel's myth gives her credit for the revolutionary abandonment of the corset, Paul Poiret – known in France and America as the 'King of Fashion' – laid claim to having abolished this article of underclothing as early as 1903. 'It was in the name of Liberty that I brought about my first revolution, by deliberately laying siege to the corset', he boasted.[7] Paul Poiret, Marie, Marthe and Regine Callot – proprietresses of the forward-looking fashion house Callot Soeurs – also rejected the corset, designing comfortable, yet elegant, evening gowns and daywear. Other designers took the lead in designing sportswear for active women. Jeanne

LA FOLIE DU JOUR

Dédié à l'occasion du 1er Janvier 1914 aux Amis du Journal des Dames et des Modes.

Fashion plate by Georges Barbier, *Journal des dames et des modes* (1914).

Paquin, head of one of the largest couture houses in Paris – with stores also in London, Buenos Aires and Madrid – sold outfits for women who golfed, motored and hunted; and she designed soft, practical day-into-evening dresses for women who would not be changing clothes several times a day. Paquin's fresh take on black dresses, and her combining of black and white, also predates Chanel's innovations.

Nevertheless, Chanel's hats – to which she soon added sweaters and sportswear – had a fresh look that intrigued many Deauville shoppers. Baroness Catherine d'Erlanger for one, a well-placed decorator, talked about the boutique to her friends. The widely read fashion report *Women's Wear Daily* noticed Chanel in July 1914, praising her 'extremely interesting sweaters which embrace some interesting features. The material employed is wool jersey in most attractive colourings as pale blue, pink, brick red, and yellow.' She also showed black-and-white and navy-and-white striped sweaters, styled like a middy blouse and sometimes belted.[8] Wool jersey from the manufacturer Rodier – purchased because it was the cheapest fabric Chanel could buy at the beginning of the war – became her signature. Yet the designs bear little resemblance to the slim, pared-down look for which she would later became renowned. In *Les Élégances Parisiennes* magazine in 1916, three Chanel outfits feature full skirts (one tiered), embroidered middy blouses with ties or belts and shoes with high heels. American *Vogue* – its French version would not appear until 1920 – showed one of her coats 'with set-in sections to widen the skirt and a deep shoulder cape to widen the top. The cuffs have amusingly pretty flaring ruffles.'[9] As a bright young fashion designer, Chanel attracted interest as much for her newness on the fashion stage as for her innovations.

Chanel's reputation was enhanced by her ability to socialize with her customers. If she had been withdrawn and reticent with Balsan at Royallieu, she was more at ease in Capel's company in Deauville and in Paris. She wanted to be more than a shopkeeper and she lit upon a new publicity strategy: she, Antoinette and Adrienne (both of whom worked for her) would be seen wearing her designs. Young and attractive, they would be living models for the clothing and hats that might otherwise only be seen in drawings in fashion magazines. They would show what it looked like to live in these clothes – at the races, in the casino, at restaurants, on the beach.

With a couture house and boutiques in Paris and Deauville, Chanel followed money – and the example of other designers – and in 1915 opened another boutique in the resort town of Biarritz, which she had first visited with Capel. On the French coast near the Spanish Pyrenees, the town had become a haven for war profiteers and rich, vacationing Spaniards. Again with Capel's financial backing, Chanel rented a villa – well-located across from the casino – and opened a larger and more lavish fashion house than the one in Deauville. She hired more than 60 seamstresses, bought fabric (including inexpensive jersey from Rodier in France) and set out her wares: sportswear, and now elegant dresses. Her prices were very expensive, even for couture, with dresses selling for 6,000 or 7,000 francs – about £218, which was half a year's wage for a typical worker. She knew, intuitively, that her customers would consider her outfits more valuable if they had to pay more. 'Costly simplicity' was often used to describe her clothing. 'Poverty deluxe', is how Poiret put it, with derision.[10]

A couturière trying to sell clothing during the war required fortitude. Fashion magazines were apologetic about the propriety of dressing up; *Femina* offered fashion advice for mourning clothes. Even in America where the effects of war were not felt daily on Manhattan's Fifth Avenue, there seemed little heart for fashion. 'A sudden gloom has fallen on Paris', *Vogue* reported in 1917. Evening gowns seemed inappropriate while soldiers were dying in Belgium; 'jewels should not be worn so long as the great guns of Verdun and the Somme need projectiles . . . It is not altogether

Chanel at Deauville in 1913.

fitting that part of Paris should disport itself at the Opera in fine raiment when another part is toiling night and day in the making of munitions.'[11] Because electricity could not be used in shops after six in the evening, boutiques were lit with candles. The result was charming, *Vogue* remarked, but for Parisians candlelight only accentuated deprivation.

Still, despite a pall caused by the war, designers offered innovations that they thought responded to women's desires: skirts were narrower but women could walk around the city easily thanks to pleats and discreet slits. Walking was necessary since petrol was rationed. 'We have walked the length of the boulevards and, to our dismay, have walked back, because of the lack of taxis', complained one of *Vogue*'s writers.[12] Wool, requisitioned for soldiers' uniforms, became scarce and expensive for designers. Instead, satin and silk returned as newly popular; capes and coats were lined with silk to keep women warm in a city with little heating fuel. Two colours prevailed in many designers' offerings: beige and grey.

In the summer of 1918 soft outfits of crêpe de Chine could hardly be distinguished from one another. Everyone, it seemed, showed loose dresses or coats, belted at or below the waist. Many designers featured embroidery, which had become popular since 1909, just after the Ballets Russes first premiered in Paris. Jeanne Lanvin's tailored suits looked like Cheruit's, and those looked like Chanel's. Charles Frederick Worth was using silk, cotton and wool jersey. Paquin had invented a bold tango dress. By the autumn of 1918 a major change in women's appearance occurred when women began to cut their hair short. The actress Irene Castle had famously bobbed her hair in 1913, but it took some years for the look to gain popularity. *Vogue* thought the style unattractive for anyone over 25 but conceded that it simplified life. Air raids, forcing women to rush into the basement in the middle of the night, and lack of hot water for bathing and washing hair, made the trend logical, if not becoming. Yet it took firm hold and fashion illustrations, always depicting younger women, now showed them with a bob and, increasingly, a cigarette.

No matter what clothes women chose to wear in Paris as the city emerged from the cold, dark winter of 1918, they accented their outfits with two tiny mascots – dangling as a pin, strung on a cord and worn as a necklace, attached to an umbrella, hanging from a handbag or tacked to a hatband. These were Nénette and Rintintin. They were dolls made of yarn and silk thread, male and female, with blue or red hair, purple or orange bodies. Nénette wore a short skirt, much like a tutu; Rintintin's short hair stood on end, in what might later be mistaken for an Afro. They had been designed by a seamstress at Paquin's as good-luck charms, 'talismans against Gothas' (German bombers), as she said. 'Have you Nénette and Rintintin?' friends would ask as they greeted one another. 'If not, beware of bombs.' Within months they were everywhere, especially on the battlefields, sent to soldiers (including American soldiers) by their French girlfriends. The war had hardly ended when the two mascots were transformed into fine jewellery: set with diamonds, attached to a platinum chain, swinging from enamelled bracelets or set in crystal lockets.[13]

It should not be surprising that after a war resulting in unprecedented casualties, many designers' first collections were predominantly black. Chanel's was no exception. Yet an ebullient spirit of renewal emerged too, even at a time of mourning. 'Paris Dines and Dances and Awaits the Openings', *Vogue* proclaimed in the spring of 1919.

Fashion magazines featured wedding dresses for two groups of women: those marrying for the first time, their grooms young officers; and those remarrying after being widowed. Soon, sections appeared with fashions for young mothers.

Couturiers, busy as they were, also worried about profits. The cost of labour had risen – even in houses like Chanel's where seamstresses, saleswomen and mannequins were notoriously underpaid – and the cost of fabrics had risen as well.[14] Year by year, the franc lost value. Once wartime restraints were removed and British and American aid withdrawn, French currency declined precipitously. Five francs to the dollar before the war became 25 francs to the dollar by the late 1920s. The depression that hit America hard in 1929 took a bit longer to arrive in France where industry had rebounded strongly after the war. But when the crisis arrived it took a big toll on industries that depended on exports, such as Chanel's company.

Besides financial pressures, Chanel was constantly aware of her competition, among whom Jean Patou was the most irritating. Just a few years older than Chanel, Patou was famous as a man-about-town and his lovers were young, attractive women – as young and attractive as Chanel. Patou was just about to open his couture house in 1914 but instead served in the war for five years. When he finally launched his business in 1919, his simple designs – incorporation of fabrics and styles from menswear – and the overall sportiness of his collections appealed to the same kind of woman that patronized Chanel.

Like Chanel, Patou did not draw, but rather than create designs on a model, he shared ideas with a team of collaborators who worked in a kind of 'laboratory' to come up with sketches. He was as mindful of Chanel as she was of him. According to *Vogue* editor Edna Woolman Chase, Patou considered Chanel his enemy and complained passionately whenever he decided that the magazine was giving too much space to Chanel. Finally, Chase threatened to withdraw all mention of him if he did not stop protesting, which elicited an apology.

Patou's gambling and womanizing eventually led to a financial crisis for his fashion house. If his socializing proved not advantageous for his business, Chanel's increasing prominence in Parisian society proved a great boon. Her standing depended not only on her relationship with wealthy men but also with one strong, domineering woman: Misia Godebska. All of Chanel's biographers agree that her personal and professional life were shaped in large measure by her intense friendship with Misia. A Polish-born émigré with artistic aspirations, Misia wanted to become a concert pianist and her teacher believed she had the talent to fulfil her dream. But when she was 21 years old, she impetuously decided to marry her cousin, the banker Thadée Natanson who founded the influential journal *La Revue Blanche*. Instantly thrust into the cultural eddies of Paris, Misia befriended such artists as Stéphane Mallarmé,

Saint-John Perse, Claude Debussy, Erik Satie, Jean Cocteau and Marcel Proust. She modelled for Vuillard, Renoir and Bonnard. Seductive, dramatic and beautiful, Misia attracted much amorous attention and Natanson began to seem increasingly dull. Soon, she became involved with the more flamboyant and rich Alfred Edwards, owner of the daily newspaper *Le Matin*. Her divorce from Natanson was fodder for gossip, as was her marriage to Edwards in 1905.

With Edwards, Misia entered into a wider world of the arts and society. She doted on Igor Stravinsky and Sergei Diaghilev; counts and barons dined at her table. But Edwards turned out to be a faithless husband and in 1909, amid much scandal, Misia divorced him. Quickly, she found a substitute: the wealthy Catalan painter José-Maria Sert. 'If one wishes to discover the woman of Paris whose attachments were the most diverse, who has known best those whom Europe honors, who has given the greatest friendship to composers, painters, poets, politicians, writers, sculptors, musicians, and men of the theatre, one would finally decide on Madame Sert', wrote Maurice Sachs, who sometimes had a place within her changing circles of friends.[15]

Misia, by all accounts, was a fury. 'She inspired genius', said the diplomat Philippe Berthelot, 'as some kings know how to produce conquerors, with the vibrancy of her being, with an almost invisible tap of her wand'. She was 'avaricious, generous, devourer of millions, cajoler, scamp, subtle, businesslike, appraising and scorning people at a glance . . . Misia, as comfortable as a sofa, but if you craved rest, that sofa would land you in hell.'[16] Paul Morand remembered her as a woman

effervescing with joy or fury, eccentric, acquisitive and a collector of geniuses . . . a collector of hearts and of Ming trees in pink quartz; whenever her latest fads were launched, they became instantly fashionable among all her followers, and were exploited by designers, written about by journalists and imitated by every empty-headed society lady.

She was brilliant but treacherous, deceitful and cruel.[17] 'All in all, Misia was a fascinating cross between an angel and a tigress', the photographer Horst P. Horst remembered. He was not alone in noticing her mercurial moods: 'Composer Erik Satie described her as "a lovely cat – so hide your fish!"; and Cocteau (whom she loved, counseled, and bossed) wrote admiringly of her "soft and cruel face."'[18] Everyone looked to her for advice, which she gave freely, often with financial help when it was needed, Horst said.[19]

By the time she met Chanel in 1917, Misia was 45 and practised doing what she did best: controlling the lives of others. Chanel at 34 was comparatively inexperienced and still, according to her own account, timidly observing, making great efforts to find her own place in Capel's world. She did not always feel accepted by the socialites among her customers. 'They greeted her in her shop', one friend remembered, 'but the women of high social position did not speak to her – at the races, for example. And this kind of behavior certainly caused her to suffer; she was marked by it for the rest of her life.'[20] She found easier acceptance among the artists, writers and actors who clustered around Misia, but even among them she felt timid and she rarely spoke. If Chanel looked to Capel for instruction, now she had another master eager for a disciple: Chanel would become Misia's project.

They may have met at a dinner party hosted by the actress Cécile Sorel – where other guests included Misia's then fiancé José-Maria Sert, Philippe Berthelot and his wife and Jean Cocteau. She may have been brought to the dinner by 'Boy' Capel, who was shuttling between London and Paris in his role as a statesman. Capel had just published a book, *Reflections on Victory*, in which he proposed a British and Allied federation for bringing about and preserving European peace. Even more significant than his writings was that he served as a liaison between David Lloyd George (the British Prime Minister) and Georges Clemenceau (Lloyd George's French counterpart) as they worked together to devise military and political strategies. In November 1917, he took the position of Political Secretary to the British delegation in France, making it possible for him to spend more time with Chanel in Paris.

It is likely that Chanel worried about their future as a couple, but it is possible she realized that they had no future together and began to withdraw her affections. Early in their affair, she recalled later, she had hoped to have a child with Capel. Those hopes though were dashed after she sought medical help in the belief that her womb was 'impenetrable'. The midwife who operated on her failed and a surgeon rushed to intervene. She learned then that she could never conceive.[21]

Yet she and Boy took responsibility for a child, the son of her sister Julia (who had killed herself when she discovered that her husband had a mistress). André Palasse was six and Capel arranged for him to attend Beaumont, the English boarding school that he had attended. André became, in a sense, the child that they could not have together. But this child could not cement their relationship and it soon ended. After almost eight years with Chanel, 'Boy' Capel met another woman: 25-year-old Diana Lister Wyndham – the daughter of Lord Ribblesdale, and a widow whose husband had been killed in an early battle. She and Capel quickly became engaged, with plans to marry quickly too. Chanel later promoted the story that she gave the marriage her blessing and even her encouragement. She apparently reimbursed Capel for the money he had loaned her, a gesture that some biographers have taken as a 'declaration of independence'.[22] But financial independence for Chanel was not related to emotional independence. She wanted to be self-sufficient, surely, but she also wanted to love and be loved.

Capel and Diana married in October 1918, and most biographers agree that he kept seeing Chanel during his engagement, after his marriage and even after his wife became pregnant. Although Chanel was seen in Paris with a wealthy Argentinean playboy, she professed an attraction for Picasso, whom she met through Misia – an attraction she insisted was reciprocated. However, she maintained throughout her life that Capel was her one true love. 'He was for me father, brother, my entire family', she told Paul Morand.[23] But the love was doomed – not only by Capel's marriage. In December 1919 Capel was killed in a car accident on the road to Cannes. Chanel, devastated, collapsed with grief. Again, she felt abandoned, just as she had been by her father; again, she suffered the emotions that overwhelmed her at the death of her mother.

Misia consoled her. Misia, she said, loved her. Misia was her only woman friend. Misia understood her and, Chanel said, craved her affection. 'This love', she explained, 'comes from a great basic generosity mixed with a devilish delight in denigrating everything she gives'. They acknowledged the mystery – and surely the duplicity – within each of them; perhaps they acknowledged, also, a deep self-hatred. 'For herself, whom she loathes, for the man she serves, her tactical knowledge and her promotional strategy are always on the alert', Chanel said of Misia.[24] She might have been describing herself.

3

À la folie

She was a general, one of those young generals of the French Empire dominated by a spirit of conquest.
Maurice Sach, 1933[1]

Euphoria followed the end of the First World War. For the next seven years, Maurice Sachs wrote, 'the shops were never emptied, the auditoriums always full, the streets crammed with visitors'. It was a time, he said,

> when everyone was a collector, not knowing what else to do with his money, and everything that was collected immediately increased in value, without great consideration of quality. Easy money caused an ephemeral effervescence in the arts, making them the subject of a rootless craze that it would later be hard to have to do without . . . it was a tacitly established law that everyone must live *à la folie*.[2]

Chanel was swept up in the madness. At 36, she was never more attractive and alluring. She seemed, said American *Vogue*, to have 'an extraordinary perception of the woman of to-day'.[3] That woman was energetic, restless, slender and young. The one adjective repeated all during the 1920s – as Chanel's reputation grew – was 'youthful'. Chanel's style, said *Women's Wear Daily*, is youthful and active in effect, just as the little Garçonne type of silk dress is youthful, and it has an out-of-doors quality that pleases a certain set of youthful Parisienne matrons who find it amusing to walk, golf, and motor à l'anglaise.[4]

Other designers, like Chanel, favoured taupe, greys and dull tans, and their dresses too were the 'youthful, short-skirted chemise type'. Like Chanel, for example, Madame Renée was popular with American buyers who praised her 'straight, low-waisted, slightly bloused and open-necked' styles.[5] In 1923, *Women's Wear Daily* determined that 'the smart woman wants to be young in silhouette, and comfortable, and has made her ideal the smartly practical'.[6]

Designers had blurred gender boundaries even before the war, incorporating men's jackets, shirts and ties into their styles. But after the war, the androgynous body became an ideal for many women. Jean Cocteau – always a loyal publicist for his friend Chanel – was one of many observers with a theory about the cause: he claimed that *haute couture* had for too long been influenced by designers like Poiret whose harem pants and embroidered tunics had seemed fanciful, whimsical and even theatrical. Poiret adorned women; he decorated them. But the war had made that kind of caprice irrelevant to real life; women no longer wanted fantasy and Chanel believed she knew what they did want. 'She was the first to understand how wearied women were and their need of being themselves once more', Cocteau wrote. 'She was the first to instigate confusion, that new order might come from it.' The confusion centred on androgyny. 'The hair must be bobbed, breasts and buttocks were to be concealed, as much as possible women must look like the young men who had protected them against the invader', Cocteau concluded. Chanel created what he called 'a *violent* simplicity' of which she served as the best model.[7] Except for this opinion, there is no evidence that women identified with soldiers, but there is evidence

Chanel, *c.* 1920.

that the war had pushed them into the marketplace and further into what *Vogue* called 'strenuous lives' of 'keen activity'.[8]

Unfortunately, noted Edna Woolman Chase, *Vogue's* editor, not all women should have been wearing Chanel's styles, 'but such was her magnetism and such the power of fashion that throughout the Twenties the most unlikely female figures deluded themselves into a sort of mirage, where, like their designer, they also moved, slender and girlish'.[9] When they looked in the mirror, they saw Chanel – glamorous Chanel, as she appeared in the photographs of fashion magazines. 'Gabrielle Chanel whose Designs are as Youthful and Chic as Herself': this was the caption in *Vogue* (both in the American and French editions) for a portrait of Chanel wearing a grosgrain ribbon hat, 'a very smart brooch and earrings of beautiful pearls'.[10] Her eyes almost completely shaded by the brim of her cloche hat, her skin flawless, her lips boldly red: she looked stunning.

Some women may have seen a mirage when they looked in the mirror but others were determined to remake their image to fit the new style. Although French *Vogue* cautioned that 'elegance is not necessarily synonymous with svelteness', many women were determined to transform themselves.[11] Corsets that pushed women into hourglass shapes were replaced by those that pressed women's bosoms and hips into slim, straight lines. Only with corsets, *Vogue* advised, could women 'acquire that much sought uncorseted effect'.[12] For some women the effect could be achieved through self-discipline, self-control and self-denial: in short, by dieting rigorously. Fashion magazines exhorted women to exert power over their minds, and by extension, their bodies. Fad diets abounded, some advising women to consume fewer than 700 calories a day.

A more drastic solution to dissatisfaction with one's body resulted in cosmetic surgery. Before the war, women could make the choice of wearing clothing that more or less concealed their bodies and whatever defects they believed they had. But post-war styles revealed busts, hips and legs. Besides wearing constricting undergarments, some women resorted to surgery to attain the long, slender leg that would be shown off as hemlines rose almost to the knee. A beautiful leg became alluring, sexy, classy. Slim, smooth calves, especially, seemed youthful. How would a woman attract a man, how would she get hired for a good job, without good legs? Cosmetic surgeons across Europe and in America found themselves confronting a new clientele: women in severe psychological and emotional distress, women who hated their bodies.

The central paradox in the craze for slimness was not that corsets could effect an uncorseted look, but that women seemed to believe that their newly diminished bodies were evidence of social and psychological freedom, that conforming to a flat-chested, small-hipped model demonstrated their individuality, and that looking like a male adolescent revealed a newly defined femininity. Certainly women believed that a pared-down body was requisite for sexual freedom: the ability to attract lovers, choose from among them and discard them. Part of Chanel's legend ascribes this sexual freedom to her, as if she took a powerful role in her love affairs, ended them when she wished, refused men's yearning proposals – all for the sake of her career, which alone brought her satisfaction. Yet, again and again, she insisted that women are happiest when they are loved. 'Few people suspect it', she told Joseph Barry when she was in her eighties, 'but I have never known happiness'.[13]

Chanel claimed that she stayed at home in the evenings and did not participate in the frenzied social life of post-war Paris, partly because of her self-proclaimed shyness, partly because she wanted to be fresh, alert and ready to work each day. Still, many witnesses attest to her presence at a variety of social and arts events, and also to her own luxurious, intimate dinners and, especially in the 1930s, her lavish parties. She had many admirers: between the death of Capel in 1919 and the beginning of her relationship with the Duke of Westminster in 1924, Chanel was involved with three men: Igor Stravinsky, the Russian exile Grand-Duke Dmitri Pavlovich and the poet Pierre Reverdy. Biographers date her affair with Stravinsky as occurring from September 1920 to May 1921; her affair with Reverdy between 1920 to 1924 and her meeting with Dmitri in 1921. The coincidence of these affairs would have kept her quite busy, and juggling meetings – since Stravinsky and Reverdy were both married – would have required

a great deal of strategy. It seems possible, then, that at least some of these relationships overlapped.

In late September 1920, Stravinsky was in Paris with his wife Katya and their four children, trying to find a place to live. Chanel – whom he had met through Misia the preceding spring – had recently bought a villa, Bel Respiro, in Garches just outside of Paris, and offered it to Stravinsky and his family while they searched for a permanent place. His affair with Chanel apparently began immediately and he claimed that he kept it secret from his family. Katya, though, is said to have tolerated her husband's many affairs, believing it her duty to support and forgive a man of genius. One of

Stravinsky's biographers speculates that Chanel and Stravinsky had their trysts at the Hotel Ritz where Chanel kept an apartment. Although she turned over Bel Respiro to the Stravinskys, it is likely that she visited now and then, and that she heard Stravinsky play *Le Sacre du Printemps*. A surprise gift of substantial money to Diaghilev, enabling him to mount a revival of the piece, coincided with the affair.

Stravinsky, as one historian described him, was 'a dandy and a womanizer'. In 1921, Diaghilev introduced him to Vera Sudeikina who endured as the longest of his lovers and eventually became his second wife (after Katya died from tuberculosis); and there were many other women, before and after Chanel. Described as short, 'with thick Slavic features', Stravinsky was 'fussy and self-conscious in his dress. He exercised daily, was muscular and fit, yet something of a hypochondriac.' He put himself on crazy diets of mostly raw vegetables, including raw potatoes. He was vain and eager for admiration, and Chanel – who said men should be treated like children – was eager to praise him, listen sympathetically to his many worries about his health, and keep him happy with gifts of clothing from exclusive shops. When he feared catching a cold because a rehearsal hall was chilly, she bought him a lambskin coat. Like his wife, she considered him a genius, deserving of indulgence.

If the liaison was secret from the family, it was hardly secret to Misia Sert. Misia was offended both because Chanel did not confide details of the affair to her and because of the affair itself. 'What are you doing? Where are you going?' she asked Chanel accusingly. Not for the last time, Misia behaved as if she were in competition with Chanel as lover of artists and patron of the arts. As Chanel recounted the affair later, Misia tried to stir up trouble in the pair's relationship by insisting to Chanel that Stravinsky was intent on divorcing Katya to marry her, and by making Stravinsky jealous in telling him that Chanel had met someone new, a Russian Grand-Duke.

Whatever hopes Chanel had for the affair, she later rendered it as a brief fling that was mutually beneficial to both parties. Chanel believed that she changed Stravinsky's life, transforming him from a shy and modest man into 'a hard man with a monocle; from a victim into a conqueror'. He gained business sense and learned to defend his artistic interests.[14] At the time, others saw him as a man fully conscious of his genius but who was able to pretend modesty; already a self-promoting, publicity-seeking individual who craved constant admiration; or he might have learned some of those behaviours from Chanel.

What did she get out of the brief liaison? Chanel claimed that everything she knew about music she learned from Stravinsky. He also affirmed her abiding faith in lucky numbers and charms. Like Chanel, he was very superstitious, often attaching amulets and religious medals to his undershirts. After a trip to America in 1925, he returned with a new – if self-serving – interest in the church. His son Soulima remembered bitterly that Stravinsky forced the family to pray in front of icons, a performance that seemed staged and insincere.[15] But for Chanel, the reverence was touching; he gave her a Russian icon, which she kept at her bedside forever. When their affair ended, Stravinsky became involved with a cabaret performer and soon after with Vera Sudeikina; and Chanel became involved with Dmitri. Stravinsky and his family left Garches in the spring of 1921.

At a party given by the opera singer Marthe Davelli, one of Chanel's earliest customers, Chanel met Grand-Duke Dmitri Pavlovich. Dmitri was the exiled Russian cousin of Tsar Nicholas, rumoured to have murdered the insidious royal advisor Rasputin. Although Dmitri admitted that he had witnessed Rasputin's murder, he claimed that he did not actually participate in the deed. Nevertheless, he believed that eliminating Rasputin's influence in the Russian court was in the country's best interest. Tsar Nicholas, however, thought otherwise and exiled Dmitri.

The story only added to his appeal: Dmitri was welcomed with enthusiasm into French high society.

Davelli told Chanel that Dmitri was her lover but – a remark repeated by Chanel's biographers – that he was becoming too expensive; she could have him if she was interested. Eleven years younger than Chanel, Dmitri at 25 was, as Consuelo Vanderbilt remembered him, undeniably attractive: 'An exceptionally handsome man, fair and sleek with long blue eyes in a narrow face, he had fine features, and the stealthy walk of a wild animal, moving with the same balanced grace.'[16] He was handsome, titled and available, and Chanel was indeed interested.

Soon Dmitri was installed in Garches, replacing Stravinsky, and for two months in the summer of 1922 the couple rented a villa overlooking the Atlantic coast. They were a beautiful pair, photographed looking romantically into each other's eyes. But Dmitri's eyes often strayed, and in 1926 – at a tea in Versailles – he met a 22-year-old American heiress, Audrey Emery, daughter of the late Cincinnati multimillionaire John Josiah Emery. Attractive

Chanel with Grand-Duke Dmitri Pavlovich, 1920.

and very rich, Audrey became the focus of Dmitri's amorous attentions and after a two-week engagement they married in the Russian church in Biarritz. Taking the Russian name of Anna, she was thereafter known as Princess Romanovsky-Ilyinsky. Attended by many members of the exiled Russian nobility, the wedding was suitably splendid; the bride's lace veil had been worn by Dmitri's mother and sister at their weddings; she carried a bouquet of white orchids; her wedding dress was by Molyneux.

Despite Dmitri's marriage, the echo of his affair with Chanel gave her a certain allure, even years later. 'The fame of Gabrielle ("Coco") Chanel has waxed since the War', *Time* magazine reported in 1928.

> Sweaters have made her name and her fortune, the light boyish sweaters which form the sports costume of many an American and English woman. The story of Gabrielle is shrouded in mystery. Some say she is of Basque origin, the daughter of a peasant. Others declare her youth was spent in Marseilles, where the jerseys of sailors gave her the idea for the emancipated woman's golfing costume. Even today she is something of an enigma to gossip-loving Paris. 'Coco' Chanel is not beautiful, yet her name is linked with that of Prince Dmitri, Parisian man of the world, famed connoisseur of beautiful women.[17]

Probably in 1920, Chanel met the enigmatic poet Pierre Reverdy at Misia's apartment in Hotel Meurice. At 31, dark-eyed, restless, spiritually and emotionally tormented, Reverdy was intensely attractive to Chanel. What she knew of him at first was what others knew: raised in southern France, where his father was a wine grower, he had come to Paris in 1910, already a poet. At the start of the First World War, unable to serve in battle because of a heart condition, he joined the auxiliary forces, which afforded him ample time to write. By the end of the war he had published eight books, including the autobiographical novel *Le Voleur de Talan* and several volumes of poetry. In order to disseminate his aesthetic theories and promote the Cubist and Surrealist writers he championed, he founded the journal *Nord-Sud* in 1917, which drew contributions from a prolific community of writers, among them Louis Aragon, André Breton and Tristan Tzara. Misia Sert helped him to find subscribers but even then it only lasted for sixteen issues; still, the journal exerted considerable influence among French avant-garde writers.

Besides Misia, Reverdy counted luminaries of Montmartre among his friends, such as Guillaume Apollinaire, Max Jacob, Picasso and Juan Gris. Among these artists and writers, Reverdy was considered a theorist, working out aesthetic principles that underlay his own poetry and the Cubist, Surrealist and Dadaist art that he published and heralded. To make a living, he worked as a proofreader for newspapers, struggling to support himself and his wife Henriette Bureau, a dressmaker. Their under-furnished attic apartment on the rue Cortot in Montmartre became icy in winter, with coal scarce during the war, and their funds even more scarce. 'I wrote in an attic', Reverdy remembered, 'where the snow, falling through the cracks in the ceiling, turned blue'.[18]

His attraction to Chanel seems surprising, but apparently he became obsessed with her, and she with him. Their relationship was volatile, sometimes explosive and ardent. Charles-Roux speculates that in Reverdy, Chanel saw 'a man of her own breed, as deeply marked by the hazards of the soil as her own people'.[19] What they had in common, however, was far more crucial to both of them than simply sharing common soil: they shared the stigma of their past. Like Chanel, Reverdy was ashamed of his origins and invented stories to hide the truth about his early life. In fact, he had been abandoned by his unmarried parents soon after his birth in 1889. Not until he was six did his father acknowledge paternity; even then, for the next two years he lived with his mother until his parents finally married. Like Chanel, Reverdy came to Paris an outsider ambitious for fame; like her, he felt the danger of being revealed. Like her, he succumbed to depression and loneliness. 'Her own secret austerity recognised its counterpart in him', Claude Delay concluded, when Chanel recounted the affair. Chanel told her that he was hard on himself but gentle with others. He longed for friendship but his frankness put people off. He would come to dine with her, bringing poems. Reading them, he said, would be like 'chewing stones'. 'He was a lofty spirit', Chanel told Delay, and he had been precious to her.[20]

Ascetic, mystical, reclusive, Reverdy professed to care nothing for the material. Even his fellow poets believed that he lived in his own world of images and sensations, detached from what André Breton called 'the things that suffuse everyday life, the halo of apprehensions and clues that floats around our impressions and our acts'. Reverdy, Breton said, 'dipped into it as if by chance'. His passion for poetry – a particular kind of obscure, hermetic poetry – was infectious and when he talked, he created a kind of 'verbal magic' that was dazzling.[21] But his personality as a poet was overcome at times by his passions as a man: he was known to drink to excess and to smoke too many cigarettes; he loved good food and ate too much of it; seductions enthralled him – just as they enthralled Chanel. Fighting against this sybaritic part of his personality, Reverdy sought spiritual enlightenment and in 1921 – prodded by his friend Max Jacob – he, along with his wife, converted to Catholicism.

Reverdy's poetry reveals a sense of emptiness and isolation that made friendship difficult. If his affair with Chanel continued until 1924, as Charles-Roux maintains, then it must have been fraught with his hopelessness. Maybe Chanel shared a sense of emptiness that her thriving career did not assuage; maybe she wanted to find a way to protect and care for her lover. Whatever her feelings, she threw herself into the affair, and was as astonished as his other friends when Reverdy announced in 1926 that he and his wife were moving to Solesmes, where he would enter the Trappist Abbey of St Peter as a lay brother. For the next two years, Reverdy remained a member of that community, publishing a collection of aphorisms on the artist's need for faith. Yet spiritual anguish persisted for him and he left the abbey – and the Catholic faith – in 1928, disillusioned and depressed. Still, he and Henriette continued to live in Solesmes, but Reverdy gave up neither his connection to urban life nor to Chanel. He sometimes took a train to Paris to visit her and, later on, stayed occasionally at her home in the south of France. Their friendship lasted until his death in 1960, a friendship that Chanel treasured. In her apartment at Rue Cambon, she displayed Reverdy's complete works – all fifteen volumes, along with the books that she had begun collecting with her newly acquired wealth.

In 1923, Chanel moved from Garches to Faubourg Saint-Honoré, where she decorated a luxurious residence with sumptuous furnishings. Although her shop was spare and simple (white walls, beige carpeting, Art Deco wall sconces), Chanel's personal living space seemed like a theatre set or a museum. In part, her choices were made with the advice of the Serts. Maurice Sachs remembered huge gilded Louis xiv chairs covered in white velvet; other antique chairs were upholstered in satin and long couches in taupe suede. Enormous bouquets of white flowers graced every room. She collected lacquered Coromandel screens with images of camellias (her favourite flower) – no matter that in France the flower was associated with courtesans and dandies; in China, the camellia was a symbol of purity. Gilt-framed mirrors hung on every wall; mirrors had been forbidden in her aunts' home, she said, and so she surrounded herself with them. Also surrounding her, within arm's reach in every room she inhabited, were totems and charms, including tarot cards and crystal balls: magical pieces to bring her luck or ward off danger. Gilt replicas of ears of wheat (symbol of prosperity) evoked her childhood in the Auvergne and the rooms were replete with lions (her astrological sign was Leo). At some point, she acquired a bust of a clergyman that eventually sat on a mantel in her dining room. She claimed that he was an ancestor – sometimes her own, sometimes 'Boy' Capel's – and always maintained that he offered her protection.

There were also shelves of leather-bound books, bought for her by Maurice Sachs (who, their mutual friend Cocteau assured her, was an experienced book buyer and appraiser). She paid Sachs 60,000 francs a month to buy rare first editions, but when Pierre Reverdy examined the purchases, he told Chanel the books were neither precious nor rare; Sachs had charged her double or triple what he paid for the books, using most of her stipend for his personal expenses. The payment to Sachs, however, was a small amount for Chanel, who had inherited £40,000 from Capel (worth about £620,000 today). By that time, Chanel had moved her flourishing business from 21 to 31 rue Cambon, a six-storey building where it remains today.

Venues for publicity doubled in the summer of 1920 when the enterprising publisher Condé Nast brought out the first issue of French *Vogue*. Under the editorship of Edna Woolman Chase (who did not speak French and who continued to edit American *Vogue*), the new magazine focused on Paris couture but also brought American and British viewpoints abroad. Many American and British socialites were featured in its society pages, along with news of their marriages. In August 1920, for example, one article imparted advice from Americans to French women about divorce. Chanel – who had been touted in American *Vogue* for years – now began to appear in the French version as well, which she watched with jealous attention, quick to note if other designers were given more space or praise.

As her fashion fame increased throughout the 1920s, Chanel presented an early opening for her February and August showings to attract foreign buyers, chief among them Americans, hoping that they would buy models to sell in exclusive clothing shops or to copy for sales in department stores. 'I admire and love America', Chanel later told Paul Morand. 'It's where I made my fortune. For many Americans . . . I am France.'[22] Department store buyers purchased far more than individual clients – hundreds of models at a time – and they paid a higher price than individual customers, insuring the couturière a firm income base and wide dissemination of the brand. For the price, the buyer received the article of clothing, which was then taken apart and used to create a pattern that would be manufactured by a domestic clothing company or even sent abroad – to South America perhaps, where labour was cheap. Sometimes, couture houses provided instructions about the type of fabric to be used, but most of the manufacturers had their own suppliers and copies only approximated the original. The higher the price for the copy, the closer it was supposed to be to the original.

Many of Chanel's simple, straight-lined outfits were easily copied, which she insisted pleased her. It was a 'great pleasure', she said, when she discovered that her designs had been 'realised by others, sometimes more successfully than me. And that is why I have always differed from my colleagues, over the years, about what for them is a great drama, and which for me does not exist: copying.'[23] Out of a few thousand *haute couture* customers worldwide, only a portion could be counted upon to purchase her models. And of these, she well knew, some would never pay: royalty, she claimed, were the worst offenders. Of the hundreds of outfits shown each season, only about 10 per cent would find any buyers at all. *Haute couture*, she was learning, did not survive on individual customers.

Still, although Chanel repeatedly said that imitation equalled flattery, she was vehemently against illegal copying, an industry that thrived in the fashion district of Paris. 'The totally mad desire which filled the world for Chanel's designs gave rise to a new angle in stealing them', one fledgling copyist, Elizabeth Hawes, remembered. She went to openings with the mission of copying designs, knowing that if she made anything other than a small move with

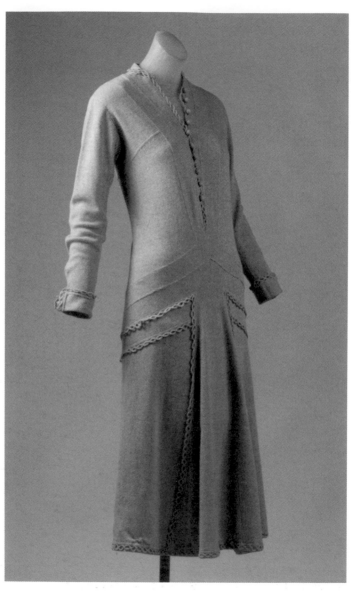

Chanel, wool dress, *c.* 1924.

her pencil, her paper would be grabbed out of her hand by one of the saleswomen posted in every corner of the room. To thwart copyists, Chanel did not provide a long programme but only small slips of paper. Models walked in and out quickly. Still, Hawes was able to copy almost an entire collection.[24] 'In New York in 1928, you could meet one lady in a Chanel she'd bought on the rue Cambon for $200', Hawes reported. Then,

> she could meet a lady who'd bought the same dress at Hattie Carnegie for $250. That lady could meet another lady who'd bought the same Chanel at Lord & Taylor for $59.50. And there were the other ladies who also bought the same Chanel, well, maybe not the same material, but the same design, for $19.75 or $10.50.[25]

Even women who sewed their own clothes could approximate a Chanel style by buying a pattern from McCall's Pattern Company, Butterick or Vogue Patterns. Apart from Lord & Taylor, copies of Chanel – or clothing imitating her designs – were available at Bergdorf Goodman, Bonwit Teller, Saks Fifth Avenue, Arnold Constable, Franklin Simon, Hollander and Gimbel's – among many other venues.

Like Chanel, Jean Patou was eager to attract American buyers. He decided that one way to do so was to hire American models to show potential clients how well his designs looked on women who were taller and more robust than the typical French. In November 1924, he placed an advertisement for mannequins and sailed for New York where, at the *Vogue* offices, he would choose a few models to take back to Paris with him. Patou was astounded when 500 women appeared, presenting themselves to a team that included socialite Elsie de Wolfe, photographer Edward Steichen, Condé Nast, Edna Woolman Chase and Patou himself. Chanel became incensed at the publicity that Patou generated when he returned with his six beautiful American models. Determined to lure them from Patou, she uncharacteristically offered them more money to join her *cabine*.

Chanel was always alert to her competitors' strategies, whether in style or marketing. Grand Duchess Marie, sister of Dmitri, met Chanel in 1921 and was impressed by her 'fierce vitality' and single-mindedness. Chanel, Marie thought, realized that success in the fashion world depended on more than dressing the elite: it should appeal to all strata of society. Marie, although in financial straits like others who had fled Russia, had an impressive pedigree: married to Prince Wilhelm of Sweden in 1908, she had divorced shortly before the First World War. After serving as a nurse in military hospitals during the war, she then married another prince, Serge Mikhailo-vitch Poutiatine, in 1917 but that marriage had ended too.

At the time they met, Chanel – like many other couturières at the time – was incorporating Slavic designs into her work. This interest in the exotic and the oriental had begun years before among fashion designers when the Ballets Russes amazed audiences with its colour-ful, extravagant costumes and sets. 'George Bernard Shaw did not stretch the truth', dance critic Carl Van Vechten wrote in 1915, 'when he said that for the past five years the Russian Ballet has furnished the sole inspiration for fashions in women's dress'.[26] The trend was abetted by the influx of Russian exiles in Paris in the late 1910s; and Chanel was also influenced by her liaison with Dmitri.

At the time she met Marie, Chanel was interested in having her silk blouses embroidered, and Marie witnessed an argument over money between the designer and the woman who had done her embroidery. Needing a way to support herself, Marie offered to embroider the blouse at a much lower price, even though at the time she knew nothing about how to embroider by machine. Within three months, however, she had mastered the craft, bought a number of machines, found a workspace and hired a staff of Russian exiles for her factory. She called her factory Kitmir, the name of a mythical dog in Persian literature.

Chanel, wool and silk ensemble, *c.* 1927.

At first, Chanel was her only customer – an arrangement that suited both women. Marie wanted steady work and Chanel wanted exclusivity. Describing Chanel's process of designing, Marie reported that she worked with an elderly and bad-tempered fitter, devoted but quick to resist her employer's ideas. Fittings were slow and painstaking. 'No one spoke except Chanel, who kept up a steady flow of monologue', Marie noted. 'Sometimes she would be giving instructions or explaining some new detail, sometimes she would criticize and undo the work that already had been done.' The fitter, silent, would meet Chanel's remarks with a glare, but no one contradicted Chanel. 'I had never yet met with a person whose every word was obeyed and whose authority had been established by her own self out of nothing', Marie admitted.

At five o'clock, coffee was brought in and Chanel would stop her work to have a cup with whichever visitors happened to be there; her monologue continued, including gossip and her opinions about everything and everyone.

> She was violent in her expressions but changed her opinions about things very easily. She went on and on without allowing anybody the time for an answer or a protest. Her statements had to be accepted.[27]

The Russian-style embroideries were very popular and Marie's business grew so large that she employed about 50 embroiderers, and a staff of designers and technicians. Chanel allowed her to do work for foreign buyers, who were charged more than Chanel, but not for French buyers, who were copying illegally. Some American buyers, too, tried to get Marie to supply embroidery on garments that were not from Chanel.

Her loyalty to Chanel was tested when other designers came to her for work. Marie wanted Kitmir to take on more clients in case Chanel went out of favour, but Chanel protested. She provided

Marie with a list of designers that she must refuse to work for, a list so impractical that Marie decided she must make a choice between working exclusively for Chanel or not. Chanel, not surprisingly, disapproved violently and their relationship fell apart. Later, Chanel claimed that she felt 'immensely sorry' for the Russian exiles who sought work in Paris; sorry but also fascinated. 'Inside everyone from the Auvergne', she said, 'there is an Oriental one doesn't realise is there: the Russians revealed the Orient to me'.[28]

Her inner Orient lasted only a few seasons and extended beyond Russia to evoke India, China and even peasant designs from Czechoslovakia. But unadorned simplicity returned as her trademark. In 1924, *Vogue* featured a white georgette evening dress, cut on the bias, with only a string belt to suggest a low waist. Sweater jackets and innovative scarves were noted features in her autumn collection, in which she favoured brown, black and taupe. Chanel's opening in April 1926 was deemed 'brilliant' by Baron Alphonse de Meyer who reported on fashion for *Harper's Bazaar*. Dominated by beige and bordeaux, her styles varied little from what her exuberant audience expected, only that year – deciding that she could 'no longer bear the sight of women's calves' – she lowered hemlines in the back, keeping the front short. She also revived her interest in horizontal stripes. In the same report extolling Chanel's genius, de Meyer called Patou's collection magnificent. Just like Chanel, he favoured muted tones – his version of beige and bordeaux was grey and rose. For evening wear, he offered sparkling, glistening pure white.[29]

By the autumn of 1926, though, Chanel took a huge stride to the forefront of *haute couture* when she presented in her collection one singularly elegant creation: the little black dress. Made of crêpe with a round neckline, long sleeves, slight blousing at the hips and a hemline just below the knees, the dress seemed to be the essence of demure taste. *Vogue* called it the 'Ford dress', suitable for everyone, bound to be a classic. Was the dress a defiant gesture against the

Chanel's 'Ford dress' published in American *Vogue* (October 1926).

prints, brocades and embroidery offered by her competitors? Was it, as some biographers have speculated, a need to see the world in black, mourning, as she still mourned for the loss of 'Boy' Capel? Was it a recognition that even grieving women would respond positively to chic style? Whatever Chanel's inspiration for the little black dress, it proved to fulfil exactly her customers' desires.

4

Double C

There's no such thing as friendship, only money – not the same thing.
Chanel[1]

Despite the admiring press and her increasing visibility as a celebrity, Chanel worried about her business. Unlike designers who created collaboratively, Chanel refused to acknowledge that she depended on anyone else for her clothing ideas. Her work on a collection began by choosing fabrics, which she saw as central to her artistry. Her suppliers would provide hundreds of samples, displaying swatches around her workroom for her consideration. She chose every piece of fabric herself, fingering every sample mindfully, twisting it, crumpling it, comparing each to the others. Once she made her choices, she would gather her forewomen in the studio to describe her ideas, refusing suggestions from her staff because she denigrated their taste. 'You're going to cut this and that. Prepare me a suit', she ordered, with gestures that indicated what she wanted, how the sleeves should be shaped and where the waist should be. 'When you've got it falling correctly, come and see me and I'll give you the trimmings', she said, concluding the meeting. According to one seamstress who worked with her, 'she had trouble expressing her wishes, for she lacked the necessary craftsmanship; this hampered her when she talked, despite her authoritative tone'.[2] Her forewomen had to be mind-readers: 'It was extremely tough on us', one confessed, because they could never produce exactly what Chanel imagined. 'Often we had to undo everything the day before, sometimes even a few hours before, a collection.'[3] Repeatedly, they took apart garments and re-stitched them, by hand of course, never able to predict her criticisms – or her rages.

Chanel's attention to her work was indefatigable and intense. 'One needs to have watched her', Claude Delay recalled, 'neck hunched with the fascination of a schoolgirl, ribboned hat on the brown curls, standing stooped slightly forward – the unflagging movement of her fingers, the shock of her passionate hand-to-hand fight with metamorphosis'.[4] She chose each mannequin herself and passed judgement on their performance each time they modelled. They needed to be beautiful, they needed to be a certain type, as close to Chanel's own physique as possible.

She repeatedly refused to call herself an artist, insisting she was a craftswoman. But she did not deny her own aesthetic sense, nor her precious instinct, nor her passion. Without evoking the word 'artist', she managed to suggest her affinity: she likened each collection to a play, admitted that in her showings she wanted to create an illusion, and boasted about her sensitivity to her audience. She often said: 'The Scheherazade is easy; a little black dress, that's very difficult.' As fashion historian Diana Crane has noted, after the First World War, designers were increasingly written about as geniuses, working alone like painters or sculptors; their design choices were analysed as if they were works of art, and their lives were mined for revelations of how their aesthetics evolved.[5] Chanel's protest against being called an artist is evidence of the cultural pressure to identify a designer as a person of singular talent, sensibility and inspiration, rather than as a businesswoman with astute perception of the market and tight control over every aspect of her couture house.

Being a businesswoman, though, was a source of her pride and justification, she thought, for her cruelty and condescension. 'She could suddenly become a veritable monster of egotism and unkindness', Lady Iya Abdy (a customer and occasional model) remembered. 'Her outbursts of anger were dreadful. Her staff, her mannequins, her best friends know something of this. She became angry with everybody.'[6] Although she quickly forgot her anger, according to Abdy, the eruptions made working conditions painful for some of her staff. She paid notoriously miserly wages but complaints were not tolerated: when mannequins pleaded for higher pay, she summarily dismissed them, advising that they become the mistresses of wealthy men. She repeatedly accused workers of stealing from her, even though she could easily see them coming and going from the workrooms. Cynical and mistrustful, she looked for opportunities to humiliate workers, and found them all the time.

From the first, her mannequins included society women who may have come to Chanel as customers. Some friends thought she hired these women to reduce them to a position of powerlessness and subservience to her. But from the days when Adrienne and Antoinette strode around Paris and Deauville in her outfits, Chanel knew how influential her mannequins could be for business. She had no wish to humiliate them, she insisted, only to publicize her designs.

If workers and even friends thought her a snob, some understood that her arrogance stemmed from a childhood of poverty, and an abiding fear that poverty could return and undermine what she perceived as her fragile world. She knew nothing about money, her own tax lawyer said, but for her it represented public acknowledgement of her talents. Another of her lawyers thought her interest in wealth reflected fear, 'the fear of not being equal to her task and of not being capable of defending herself in a man's world'.[7] In either case, she simply could not be rich enough.

Besides clothing, she extended her business to fabrics and costume jewellery. In these enterprises she relinquished some control and allowed others, of whose taste she approved, to contribute. Count Étienne de Beaumont, Lady Sybil Colefax and Elsie de Wolfe all were early jewellery designers. Like her fashions, her jewellery was also copied by retail stores whose advertisements promoted her name. As for fabrics, about which she was so exacting, she brought in Ilia Zdanévitch (known as Iliazd), an artist whom she met through Misia. Iliazd's aesthetic sense seemed so close to her own that she made him her fabric designer in 1927 and appointed him the factory director of Tissus Chanel in 1931. Iliazd had arrived in Paris six years before, when he was 27 years old, already an outspoken futurist whose passions, besides art, were for mathematics and history. Apart from his work with Chanel, he became a noted publisher of illustrated books by such renowned artists as Georges Braque, Max Ernst, Alberto Giacometti and Joan Miró. A volume of his own poetry, *Afat*, 76 sonnets illustrated with six engravings by Picasso, was dedicated to Chanel. Complicated and sometimes abrasive, Iliazd nevertheless shared Chanel's perfectionism; when his son was born – he married a Nigerian princess in 1942 – Chanel became his godmother.

Even though businesses – her own included – thrived after the war, the continuing devaluation of the franc rattled many, and Chanel was not alone in looking for ways to increase profits. Perfume, she decided, would help. After all, other designers had their own scents and she was determined to join their ranks. Ernest Beaux, a Russian chemist whom Chanel met through Dmitri and his sister, took up the challenge of creating a scent to her specifications: feminine but not floral, abstract and mysterious. Chanel did not want her perfume to be identified with any particular flower, but instead, she insisted, to be something completely artificial. This desire for something artificial has been touted as Chanel's stroke of genius, but her rationale is curious and bewildering. She definitely wanted something different from what others offered – Poiret's flowery Bosquet d'Apollon and Aladdin, for example, scents in his collection Les Parfums de Rosine. She wanted both the scent and packaging to be new, unlike the ornate, encrusted Victorian vials or the sinuous Art Nouveau bottles that appeared on many women's dressing tables.

She said that a woman should smell like a woman and not like a rose; she insisted that a scent should not be intended to cover up poor hygiene – she was always sensitive to body odour and what she called filth – but to enhance a woman's own natural scent. She claimed to have a remarkable sensitivity to odours: 'In the lily of the valley they sell on the 1st of May', she boasted, 'I can smell the hands of the kid who picked it'.[8] She wanted, she said, 'a perfume such as never before been made. A woman's perfume with a woman's scent.'[9] Her explanations about what she wanted, and why, are so vague and contradictory as to be meaningless, and yet they have persisted as part of the Chanel myth: her perfume would revolutionize the way women smelled, just as her designs revolutionized the way women dressed.

The inventive Beaux came up with a series of scents, experimenting with scores of chemicals – including benzyl acetate and jasmine extract – which produced scents that did not fade as most did, but which contained and evoked jasmine, ylang-ylang, vetiver, sandalwood and vanilla. He numbered his experiments 1 to 5 and 20 to 24, as they were listed in Chanel's first perfume catalogue. Bound in black grosgrain and printed on rough beige paper, the catalogue looked like a poetry chapbook. No. 5 pleased her, its description as evocative as she had hoped – 'a bouquet of abstract flowers of indefinable femininity and a mythic elegance'.[10] Beaux's creation was the start of the business that would support Chanel for the rest of her life.

The choice of No. 5 as the name of the perfume has itself inspired myth. The number evokes both mystical and natural allusions: five elements (water, fire, earth, wood, metal); five senses; five oceans; five fingers on each hand; five points to a star; five pillars of Islam and five daily prayers; five lines in a musical staff; five chapters

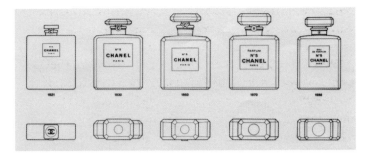

Evolution of the bottle for Chanel No. 5.

of the Torah; and for the Pythagoreans, five is a sacred number symbolizing harmony. If Chanel was thinking of any of these connotations, she never said so. Chanel No. 5 seems simply to have been Beaux's fifth sample. After the perfume's immediate success, though, Chanel took '5' as one of her lucky numbers: her showings thereafter occurred on the fifth of the month.

Chanel publicized her perfume by offering clients a small sample bottle and spraying the fitting rooms with it. When women inquired about the scent, Chanel demurred, claiming that she hardly remembered where she had found the new perfume . . . maybe somewhere in the south of France. Finally, when Beaux supplied her with enough bottles to sell, she pretended that it was her customers who urged her to produce it. What could they do but buy it?

The scent alone may have been enough to distinguish Chanel No. 5 from other perfumes, but the packaging was surely brilliant: a square bottle – imitating the vials that 'Boy' Capel had used for his colognes – with Chanel's name in black capital letters on the label and double, interlaced Cs on the cap. Sleek, modern, sophisticated, the perfume bottle marked the first appearance of the Chanel logo. With sales that far exceeded her couture sales, No. 5 – and the many fragrances that followed – made Chanel's distinctive label known to a wide and diverse international audience. Even a saleswoman making one franc an hour could possibly afford 35 francs for a 7 ml bottle of perfume, or even less for the cologne, and by dabbing it frugally she could make it last a year or more.

Chanel had learned the fashion business but marketing perfumes required a different kind of expertise, and it is likely that Chanel first approached Théophile Bader, the owner of Galeries Lafayette, where she had purchased the straw boaters that she sold as a milliner. At 60, Bader was not immune to Chanel's allure but he never lost his keen business sense. A perfume offered by the popular House of Chanel had significant sales potential, and it needed to be manufactured, packaged and distributed by someone who knew the market. That someone, Bader thought, was his friend Pierre Wertheimer who with his brother Paul ran his family's firm, Bourjois – one of the largest cosmetics and fragrance manufacturers in France.

Bourjois – originally a theatrical make-up company – was bought by Ernest Wertheimer, the patriarch, in 1898. The Bourjois plant was located in Pantin, outside of Paris, where perfume and make-up were manufactured. For example, lipstick 'batter', which came in three shades – light, medium and dark red – was cooked in large vats and stirred by hand. Each shade was poured into metal tubes that looked like shell casings, with a lever that pushed the lipstick up as the wearer used it; turning mechanisms were introduced later in the 1920s.

Chanel and Wertheimer met, so the story goes, at Deauville, where Wertheimer may have been watching one of his own many horses race; Chanel was charmed by the handsome young man and he may have been charmed by her too. She told him she wanted financial help to fund her perfume enterprise, and she found Wertheimer eager to take on the manufacture and marketing of Chanel No. 5. They would need to form a company, Wertheimer told her, a proposition to which she readily agreed. Les Parfums Chanel was established in 1924, with stipulations that she regretted for the rest of her life: she gave Wertheimer 70 per cent of the company, allotting 20 per cent as a commission to Bader and leaving only 10 per cent for herself. The fashion house remained as a separate company. The agreement seems astonishing in the light of Chanel's drive to become richer and richer, and it suggests that either she misunderstood the contract, or she did not know the earning potential of anything but couture. Later, she admitted to Claude Delay that whenever she was with businessmen she kept quiet: 'I musn't let them see I don't understand a word of what they're talking about.'[11]

Other than the division of profits, Les Parfums Chanel also had the right to market make-up and skin care products, a provision to which Chanel sometimes found reason to object. When Wertheimer decided to produce a cleansing cream, Chanel sued. Negotiations lasted for five years, ending in her defeat. In 1928, *Vogue* ran a full-page advertisement displaying 30 products with the Chanel label, including skin lotion, anti-wrinkle *gelée*, night cream for hands and face, rouge, powders and lipsticks in seven different shades. Chanel's lawsuit to stop this proliferation of cosmetics was the first of many: she tried to prohibit the company from manufacturing other perfumes; she tried to find a rival company to introduce another line herself; she tried to wrest a larger share than the 10 per cent of what – she quickly realized – would be a fortune. Chanel engaged her own lawyers and accountants to do battle with the Wertheimers, convinced that they were trying to swindle her. For their part, the Wertheimers had a team of lawyers whose sole task was to deal with Mademoiselle.

Contradicting Chanel's anxiety about money and paranoia about being cheated was her enormous and idiosyncratic generosity. 'As soon as she had money', Marcel Haedrich noted, 'she wanted to pay for everything and everyone. As people had paid for her? No: to forget that people had paid for her. Or, in somewhat harsher terms: by paying others' obligations she obliterated her own.'[12] Some of this largesse was directed at the Serts with whom she often travelled. On their trips together, her paying was one of the ways she could exert her power over them, to ensure that they would feel indebted. Dependency and indebtedness seemed to have made her feel needed and appreciated, and perhaps even loved, but her generosity was cut short for her own family. Although she frugally supported her brothers Alphonse and Lucien as her business thrived, she summarily cut them off in 1939 when she shut her doors. Contributions to family were not public, after all, and their dependency was only a burden.

She told Haedrich that she had her 'defences' against people who disliked her, or against those she perceived to dislike her.[13] One of those defences may have been money and its power to manipulate and to ensure that she was noticed. Even her tips, she told Claude Delay, were intended not as rewards but so servants would 'feel a bit of affection for you instead of spitting in your eye'.[14] Friends recount extraordinary gifts: if a woman admired a fur, she might have found it draped around her shoulders as a gift, or she might have felt a jewel pressed into her hand.

Two famous beneficiaries of Chanel's munificence to artists were Diaghilev and Cocteau. Early in 1924, after the death of his lover Raymond Radiguet, Jean Cocteau took refuge in Monte Carlo, invited by Diaghilev, whose uneven friendship with Cocteau had begun more than a decade before. Cocteau's description of Diaghilev is more satirical than affectionate: with one white shock of hair not dyed black, Diaghilev, Cocteau wrote, 'stuffed himself into a fur-lined coat with an opossum collar, and sometimes fastened it with safety pins. His face was a mastiff's, his smile a baby crocodile's, one tooth always outside. Sucking that tooth was the sign that he was pleased, or frightened, or angry.'[15] After a performance of *Les Noces* the year before, Cocteau and Diaghilev were among Gerald and Sara Murphy's fashionable guests on their yacht to celebrate the Ballets Russes. Chanel was there too, along with a host of avant-garde artists.

Hoping to distract Cocteau from his grief by engaging him in work on new ballets, Diaghilev invited him to sit in on rehearsals of the Ballets Russes, particularly so that he could see his favourite dancer: Anton Dolin. This was the dancer, Diaghilev told Cocteau, whom he wanted to feature in a new ballet. With opium helping to alleviate his grief, Cocteau felt ready to return to work. Watching Dolin's graceful athleticism, he hatched the idea of an effervescent ballet showing playtime at the seashore, and so *Le Train Bleu* was born. Cocteau called it an operetta without words, a dance piece that borrowed from mime, slapstick and circus performers. Diaghilev commissioned Darius Milhaud to write the score, with melodies drawn from popular songs and the French music-hall. 'It is Paris, vulgar, dirty, and sentimental', Milhaud wrote in his diary, 'with many polkas, galops, waltzes, etc. . . . I am a little frightened [of all the work] but I am very amused by the whole adventure.'[16] The adventure involved artists who more or less understood Cocteau's aim of creating a piece that was satirical, sophisticated and exuberant. He was not sure if Bronislava Nijinska, the sister of Vaslav Nijinsky, was a strong choice as choreographer since she knew nothing about sports or acrobatics, but he showed her photographs of the Prince of Wales playing golf and photographs of several tennis players – including Suzanne Lenglen, who triumphed at Wimbledon each year from 1919 to 1925 – whose tennis costumes were famously designed by Patou.

French sculptor Henri Laurens was commissioned to design the set to which Diaghilev added, as a front curtain, an enlarged copy of Picasso's dramatic drawing of two toga-draped women running on a beach. And Chanel, who had designed costumes for Cocteau's adaptation of *Antigone* two years before and who agreed to back the production financially, was asked to design the costumes: bathing suits, seen on stage for the first time, as well as sporting outfits – striped sweaters and socks for men, short tunics for women – for golf, tennis and tumbling. Often taking *Le Train Bleu* from Paris to the Riviera, she knew well the spirit and ambience that Cocteau was trying to convey. She knew, also, that the publicity she would gain would benefit business.

When *Antigone* opened at the tiny Théâtre de l'Atelier on 20 December 1922 (along with a short play by Luigi Pirandello), Chanel's costumes, Picasso's sets and Arthur Honegger's music all garnered attention. Cocteau claimed he chose Chanel because she was the greatest couturière and he wanted to be sure that Oedipus's daughters were beautifully dressed. Man Ray took photographs of Chanel's costumes and Georges Lepape did drawings of them for French *Vogue*, where her designs earned accolades.[17]

Rehearsals for *Le Train Bleu* were tense, partly because of long-standing enmity between Cocteau and Nijinska, heightened by their lack of a common language; partly because Cocteau pressed for more acrobatics while Nijinska tried to create a narrative in what seemed to her a series of vacation postcards. Dolin became worried about his performance as Nijinska made many last-minute changes. Serge Lifar, one of the troupe's youngest dancers, competed with Dolin for Diaghilev's attentions. At one rehearsal that was attended by Misia, Chanel and Picasso, Lifar's talents evoked spontaneous praise: 'There's your dancer', Chanel remarked to Diaghilev, and Picasso agreed. 'From then on', Lifar said, 'Coco Chanel and Picasso became my godmother and godfather in art'.[18] Chanel was there, however, not only out of curiosity. Although her costumes were innovative and lively, they fell apart quickly, and dancers could not always move in them. In fittings at the rue Cambon, Chanel did not account for stretching and leaping, so it was that she found herself during rehearsals sitting on the floor, needle in hand, repairing seams.

Le Train Bleu opened at the Théâtre des Champs-Elysées on 20 June 1924. Reviewers applauded the energetic dancing of 'chicks' and 'gigolos' cavorting on the beach, and although the choreography seemed to bear little relation to classical ballet, its gaiety and sophistication proved a crowd pleaser both in Paris and London, where performances often were sold out.

By the time the ballet opened, Cocteau was addicted to opium and continued to feel emotionally weak and depressed. His meeting with philosopher Jacques Maritain led him to embrace Catholicism, the religion in which he had been raised; and in 1925, he entered a clinic to attempt to conquer his addiction. But soon after his release, he again started smoking opium, writing paeans to 'wings of smoke' at the same time that he was extolling his faith in God. In 1928, he entered a clinic in Saint-Cloud for another try at sobriety – this time paid for by Chanel.

As Chanel socialized with artists, she discovered that it was very chic to have one's portrait done. In the early 1920s, she met the young sculptor Jacques Lipchitz and commissioned him to do a bust. She must have agreed that he captured what he called 'her strange beauty and something of her strong personality' because she later gave him other commissions: for two sets of andirons for her fireplaces, as well as for garden sculpture. Although the sculpture never materialized, Lipchitz said that the relationship was fruitful to him in opening up some new artistic possibilities.[19] A few years later, Chanel decided to commission another portrait, this time by French artist Marie Laurencin. Most sitters – knowing Laurencin's work – understood that the result would not be an exact likeness but a somewhat whimsical interpretation. Chanel apparently did not have the same understanding. When she saw that Laurencin depicted her draped in black and blue, with an elongated face and languid air, a dog perched on her lap and a bird flying near her head, Chanel was incensed. Laurencin (who characterized Chanel as a peasant from Auvergne) refused Chanel's demand to paint another portrait. Instead, with a few changes, she sold the portrait to another woman as her own likeness.

Chanel was not alone among couturiers in her support of the arts. Fashion historians note a changing perception of clothing designers, especially women designers, after the First World War. Couturiers in the early years of the century were generally trained as seamstresses and apprentices before opening their own houses; even as head of their own businesses, they were treated like tradespeople by their upper-class customers. Jeanne Lanvin (sixteen years older than Chanel) began as a milliner, and although she headed an important business, her social status rose only through the marriage of her daughter to the Comte de Polignac. Madeleine Vionnet (seven years older than Chanel) worked for one of the designers at Callot Soeurs before striking out on her own; successful enough to have shops on Manhattan's Fifth Avenue and in Biarritz, she herself was a retiring and reticent woman who hardly granted interviews, much less appeared at galas. Although both women evolved into well-regarded and popular designers, fashion magazines rarely showed photographs of them or followed their social lives, which seemed irrelevant to their creations – instead, magazines noted the celebrated women who wore their designs.

Chanel, however, took the example of Poiret and Patou who mingled socially with their clients and she pioneered a new image: a woman who travelled in the same circles as her customers, who appeared at the same events, who threw fabulous parties that her customers attended and who participated – as designer and as patron – in the world of the arts. More than merely a couturière, she became a fashion celebrity.

5

Sporting Life

She is vy agreeable – really a gt & strong being fit to rule
a man or an Empire.

Winston Churchill to his wife, 1 October 1927[1]

In 1924, Chanel was 41 years old and she had lost at least five
lovers: Balsan, Capel, Stravinsky, the Grand-Duke Dmitri and
Reverdy. Defenders of the Chanel myth insist that it was she who
left Balsan and discarded Dmitri, and that it was she who did not
want to marry, or ever to make the choice between her work and a
man. But many who observed her relationship with Hugh Richard
Arthur Grosvenor, second Duke of Westminster, portray a woman
in love, yearning for a charming, passionate and powerful man to
protect her.

The Duke was 46 years of age and his second wife, Violet Mary
Nelson, to whom he had been married for five years, had just filed
for divorce on the grounds of adultery. Over six feet tall, blue-eyed,
energetic and unconventional, the Duke was known to his friends
as Bend'Or – the name of his grandfather's stallion, winner of the
Derby in 1880 when young Hugh was fifteen months old. By the
time he reached adulthood, the nickname had transmuted into
'Bendor' for some, and even 'Benny' for close friends such as
Winston Churchill.

As his third wife, Loelia Ponsonby, described him, the Duke was
formidable, demanding and frightening: 'a czar, a sultan, a Jove

hurling thunderbolts, a deity whom I was extremely anxious to placate and whom it was quite out of the question to treat as an equal'.[2] He was easily bored and just as easily distracted – by a prank, a visitor, or the discovery of a wild flower. He was used to having everything go his way, every whim fulfilled. Even a sympathetic biographer characterized him as difficult:

> His mercurial temper, his sudden rages, his occasional unthinking cruelty to subordinates and his childish jokes, all took some getting used to, and the uncertainty of his moods meant that one minute's petulance could as suddenly be the next one's good humour.[3]

He seemed pathologically restless, hating to be alone and just as suddenly hating the company in which he found himself; his impetuous decisions to leave one place and go elsewhere were always obeyed instantly by his staff. He loved to hunt and fish on one or another of his many country properties; sail on his yacht the *Flying Cloud*; throw lavish parties; and carry on affairs with attractive, exciting women. Despite claiming to be puritanically repulsed by adultery, despite being subject to jealous rages if he suspected that he was being betrayed, he seduced countless women. The affairs contributed to the end of his first marriage to Constance Edwina Cornwallis-West, known as 'Shelagh', as well as to the end of his second. His charm and his wealth made him irresistible to some women, as well as to a cadre of sycophants and parasites who strived to get close to him.

For Chanel he offered something more than riches and jewels: protection. 'I was lucky to have known the Duke', she told interviewer Joseph Barry.

> He was shy and timid, too, but I have never felt more protected. He was solid and comfortable. He understood me – except for

my working, of course. He gave me peace. He was generous.
He was simple.

Although many who knew Chanel claimed that she was an
exhibitionist, she said she admired the Duke for not wanting to
be conspicuous. Instead of going on shore in his yachting clothes,
for example, he would change into something plain, and even worn.
He wore a pair of shoes so long that they had been repeatedly
resoled and patched. 'I detest elegant men!' Chanel remarked,
even though many of the men she befriended – Cocteau, Horst,
Serge Lifar, Dalí, Luchino Visconti – were quite elegant.[4]

It was obvious to her, of course, that the Duke was the richest
man in England, with houses and properties all over Europe,
including three hunting lodges in Scotland and two in France;
seventeen Rolls-Royces in his garage at Eaton Hall – his huge estate
in Cheshire, whose gardens covered more than 40 hectares (99 acres);
private railway cars; and two yachts: the 62-m (203-ft) *Flying Cloud*
(one of the 30 largest sailing yachts in the world) and the even larger
steam yacht *Cutty Sark*. One chronicler reported that when the
Duke went cruising in the Mediterranean, a fleet of Rolls-Royces
followed on land to cater to his needs when he stopped at any
port.[5] His gifts were breathtaking: diamonds, emeralds, sapphires,
pearls, silver and gold. Yet as Chanel remembered him later, it was
not his wealth, she said, but his simplicity and 'delightful tempera-
ment' that impressed her: 'He's a corpulent chap, heavy, robust,
at least on the outside. His intelligence lies in his keen sensitivity.'
He took pleasure in teasing, and he was not above harbouring
grudges, 'petty, elephant-like grudges'. Although she acknowledged that he could behave childishly and had a ferocious temper,
her reminiscences of his gentleness and reticence contrast sharply
with portraits drawn by others who knew him. He was a notorious
womanizer and yet she felt special, convincing herself that he was
attracted to her because unlike English women she did not pursue

him. 'If you have a very famous name and are immensely rich, you stop being a man and become a hare, a fox', she said.[6] She did not run after him but she was dazzled.

According to Loelia, though, Chanel's allure for the Duke may have been her relative obscurity, at least in his own world of titled aristocracy. 'He only liked what he called Real People', Loelia wrote. 'Apart from a few exceptions chosen by himself, nobody well known in the world or having the misfortune to have a title could be a Real Person however charming or intelligent they might be . . . The password into the Real Person Club was Obscurity.'[7] The few exceptions included Winston Churchill, with whom Bendor served during the Boer War, and depending on how we understand his perception of Chanel, perhaps Chanel herself. She was certainly among the most glamorous women of the time.

They met in Monte Carlo through her British friend Vera Bate who was working for Chanel as a publicist – with duties that included attending parties, balls and other social occasions wearing Chanel's designs, and making sure that her wealthy friends noticed. The Duke was quick to notice Chanel who in her early forties was undeniably attractive with a smile that lit up her face and a stylishness that made her stand out even among the Duke's wealthy, bejewelled guests; she looked far younger than her age. Bendor asked Bate to bring Chanel to dinner aboard the *Flying Cloud*, but Chanel – who was still involved with Dmitri – needed some persuasion to accept the invitation. After Dmitri unexpectedly turned up, Chanel agreed to go only if he was invited too. Dinner, dancing and gambling made for a long night, and by the end of it the Duke was entranced. He told Chanel he wanted to see her again.

From the beginning, Bendor may have only seen Chanel as a dalliance; but if he ever had thoughts of making her the third Duchess of Westminster, age was a decisive factor. He wanted, he needed, a son. With his first wife, he had three children: Ursula,

Edward and Mary; but Edward died of complications following an appendectomy at the age of four. That loss was devastating for the 29-year-old Duke – both emotionally and, for the future of his estate, financially. Grief turned to bitterness and anger, and he directed the anger at his wife, whom he accused of neglecting their son's health. Soon after she became pregnant with their third child, he stopped sleeping with her. By the time his daughter Mary was born in 1910, the marriage was effectively over. Without a son, his fortune would be inherited by an elderly cousin, for whom the Duke had no affection. Besides enlisting lawyers and agents to protect his estate through a trust, the Duke was intent on producing an heir.

Between his first marriage to Shelagh and his second to Violet, Bendor had several notorious affairs: with musical comedy star Gertie Millar, with ballerina Anna Pavlova and allegedly with courtesan Caroline Otero. He seemed to prefer petite, dark-haired, vivacious women; Violet was the prototype. Some of his affairs overlapped, causing distress for the woman who discovered that

Chanel with the Duke of Westminster, 1928.

she had been betrayed. Many more women, brief flings, cruised with him on his yachts; if they became seasick, they were not asked again. Bendor conducted all of his pursuits in the same way: impetuous attraction was followed by overwhelming attention, in the form of flowers, jewellery and other extravagant gifts.

The day after they met, Chanel's hotel suite in Monte Carlo filled with bouquets as the Duke began an insistent courtship. When she returned to Paris, more bouquets (including orchids) were delivered to her house, along with baskets of fruit and salmon caught on one of the Duke's Scottish estates. He wanted to, and he would, see her again. She said that she hesitated to give in to his advances, although it is hard to imagine. Quickly enough, she assented; and so she began her British period, travelling to one or another of the Duke's estates in England, Scotland or France; boarding one of his yachts; and translating his style into her own.

Newspapers took note, beginning in 1925, with reports that 'the Paris dressmaker' Gabrielle Chanel had been seen at Eaton Hall, on the Riviera and on the Duke's splendid yacht, and even that the Duke had refitted the yacht – at a cost of one million dollars – in preparation for their marriage. 'Mme Chanel Duke's Guest' announced a headline in the *New York Times* in November 1928. 'The seductive Mlle Chanel', as the newspaper referred to her, inspired juicy gossip.[8]

Just as Russian styles and embroidery characterized her clothing during her affair with Dmitri, tweeds and sportswear gained new prominence in her designs beginning in 1925. She commissioned a fabric company to weave tweed to her specifications and she claimed that she could tell instantly, forever after, whether a fabric actually was made with water from the River Tweed. Colours in her new collections were inspired by horse blankets, *Harper's Bazaar* noted, and skirts were pleated for easy movement. Sweaters and vests were shown over blouses, styled like men's shirts.[9] In 1927, a fashion illustration in *Vogue* France, set at Longchamp, depicted several socialites wearing tweed; and photos of Chanel appeared, too, dressed in sweaters, trousers and hiking boots.[10]

Winston Churchill met Chanel – 'The famous Coco', as he put it – in January 1927 when she joined the Duke for some hunting at the Château de Woolsack in Mimizan, a remote spot in southwest France. Churchill 'took a gt fancy' to her and found her 'a most capable & agreeable woman – much the strongest personality Benny has yet been up against'.[11] He was impressed by her energy: after hunting all day, she was driven back to Paris and her work. As he understood it, she needed to have 200 models ready in three weeks, some of which would be altered as many as ten times. The next autumn, Churchill and Chanel met again at Stack Lodge, another of the Duke's retreats, this one on the River Laxford in northern Scotland, teeming with salmon. Now, instead of hunting, they were fishing, with Chanel trouncing her companions. 'She fishes from morn till night', Churchill wrote to his wife, '& in 2 months has killed 50 salmon . . . Bennie vy well & I think extremely happy to be mated with an equal – her ability balancing his power.'[12] It may be that Bendor was amused by Chanel's forthrightness, but according to Loelia he could not stand the idea that any woman was his equal. Accused of trying to dominate him, Loelia faced not only his wrath but the threat of divorce.[13]

Chanel understood more English than people thought, and she took English lessons in secret with one of the Duke's secretaries. Bendor was not interested in her learning English, sure that she would become dismayed by the trivia of conversations around her; but for Chanel, bilingualism made good social sense, and business sense, too. Business, after all, was never far from her mind. She claimed later that she had been supremely bored by English country life, that the Duke baulked at her working as much as she did and that she felt the strain of his distress. But these admissions came later, after they had ended their relationship, and after he had married someone else.

Patou, silk ensemble, 1929.

Chanel in a jersey sweater and skirt in 1928.

Meanwhile, the Duke continued to shower Chanel with gifts, the most visible of which was La Pausa. According to one of the Duke's biographers, Chanel bought La Pausa with her own money in 1928; her name is on the deed of sale, dated 9 February 1929.[14] But others insist that Bendor paid 1.8 million francs to the Mayen family of Roquebrune-Cap-Martin for the two hectares overlooking the bay of Menton. To design her residence, Chanel engaged 26-year-old Robert Streitz, an architect who had been recommended to her. She did not yet have a specific idea for the villa so Streitz drafted a proposal, which pleased both Chanel and the Duke. After approving the proposal, Chanel announced – not surprising to anyone who knew her – that she wanted to be involved in every step of the process. Her desires were exacting. According to Streitz, Chanel wanted a large stone staircase, reproducing the one she remembered at Aubazine. Streitz travelled to the orphanage to photograph it. Although the land was solid rock with clay pockets,

Chanel insisted that the contractor, Edgar Maggiore, construct a massive foundation; to make the villa seem very old, she insisted that handmade, curved tiles be used for the roof, which required extensive searching for the 20,000 tiles needed. The shutters had to be aged, as well. During the construction, she came to Roquebrune once a month, taking *Le Train Bleu* to Monte Carlo, and then a taxi to the site.

The Mediterranean villa consisted of three wings, each facing an inner patio paved with 100,000 sand bricks. Inside, the floors and panels were oak. Each room had a large fireplace, with central heating only in the grand hallway. Bedrooms had balconies, and a patio stretched along three sides of the house. Dark green blinds kept out summer sun and thick walls retained heat in winter. The colour scheme throughout was predominately beige. Outside, Chanel ordered twenty 100-year-old olive trees to be transplanted from Antibes. With special fittings, decorations and landscaping, the final cost far exceeded the six million francs that the construction cost.

Unlike her Baroque apartment on the rue Cambon, the house in Roquebrune was the epitome of simplicity. In the entrance hall there were several leather-covered settees and oak refectory tables. In the white-walled living room, three large sofas flanked a huge hearth; soft, thick rugs from Spain were arranged on the oak floors; and beige silk Venetian curtains hung at the tall windows. Oak tables, a grand piano and parchment-shaded lamps were the only other furnishings. Guests could retreat to deep armchairs in the oak-shelved library, to the patio, the gardens, or to their own airy bedrooms. Only Chanel's bedroom – draped in beige taffeta, with a taffeta-quilted bedspread and an ornate headboard of scrolls and stars – departed from the austerity of the rest of the house.

She kept the house filled with tuberoses, lavender and irises from her own garden. In the central patio an olive tree provided some shade; the vestibule was always cool and welcoming. Servants

were invisible: only when she rang for coffee were they invited to
appear. Otherwise, guests served themselves from a buffet for each
meal. Chanel usually did not appear until lunch, or even later.

Bendor converted one of the three buildings on the property
to a studio where he painted watercolours. And another building
became a guest house – where Cocteau went several times to recover
from addiction or typhus. The Duke had his own suite of rooms
next to Chanel's. Vera Bate and her second husband, Alberto
Lombardi, lived in a small house on the property.

With Chanel's reputation ascendant, her friendship with Misia
shifted. No longer did Chanel need Misia's instruction and advice;
now Misia needed her. Misia, not Chanel, had been abandoned;
Misia, not Chanel, was in grief. In August 1929, Misia joined Chanel

on Bendor's yacht, taking refuge after her divorce from Sert and his remarriage to twenty-year-old Roussadana Mdivani. Misia adored Sert and she had allowed Roussy, as the young woman was called, to move into their house, taking a loving, even maternal, interest in her. She was certain that Sert would never divorce her; in fact, she was sure he *could* not, since they had been married in the Catholic Église Saint-Roch. But Sert, armed with one French and one American lawyer, managed to have their marriage annulled. Once Misia realized that Sert was going ahead with his plans, she convinced herself that all she wanted was his happiness, which she assumed must include her continued participation in his life. When Sert and Roussy invited her to join them on an Aegean cruise, she accepted. It soon dawned on her, however, that she was not really wanted and, saddened, she turned to her friend Chanel.

The *Flying Cloud* was sailing off the coast of Yugoslavia when Chanel and Misia received news that Diaghilev was gravely ill. They rushed to Venice where they found him attended by his secretary Boris Kochno and Ballets Russes dancer Serge Lifar. Diaghilev had recently come from Germany, where physicians diagnosed his aches and weakness as rheumatism; but now he had grown much worse and his two Italian doctors were not sure what was wrong with him. His back hurt, he could not eat, he was too weak to walk. After several days of being treated with various medicines and massage, his fever kept rising alarmingly, reaching 41°C (106.8°F). Bendor sent two doctors from the yacht but they too were puzzled; perhaps, they thought, it was typhoid. In fact, it was neglected diabetes causing grave problems.

With Misia and Chanel at his bedside he seemed to improve, at least enough to communicate with his visitors. By the end of the afternoon, Misia decided to stay in Venice, while Chanel returned to the yacht. But the next day she was overcome with fear for her friend and asked the Duke to turn back. As soon as she arrived in Venice, she discovered that Diaghilev had died that dawn. With

Misia, Lifar, Baroness Catherine d'Erlanger and Kochno, Chanel joined the procession of gondolas that took Diaghilev's coffin, covered with flowers, to the cemetery on the island of San Michele. She paid for the funeral. Her loyalty to Diaghilev may have inspired her to join Cole Porter and others in supporting Boris Kochno when he and George Balanchine formed their own dance company, Les Ballets, in 1933.

When she returned to the yacht after Diaghilev's burial, her relationship with the Duke began to deteriorate. The Duke may have resented her attentions to another man, even though she was not romantically involved. If Chanel showed grief over the loss of Diaghilev – a man she called 'the most delightful of friends', whose zest for life she loved, whose brilliance she extolled[15] – Bendor is likely to have erupted into a jealous rage. They may have quarrelled because the Duke disparaged Diaghilev's art, just as he disparaged any modern art. 'Anything that he did not understand filled him with rage and hatred', Loelia recalled. 'All forms of modern music, painting and sculpture were intolerable and he would have liked personally to destroy them.'[16]

Chanel, of course, may have instigated a quarrel, fed up finally with Bendor's womanizing. Often unfaithful to Chanel, Bendor's affairs made her jealous and humiliated. It may be that she refused to tolerate his infidelities, made apparent when he once brought a young woman onto his yacht while Chanel was on board. She insisted that her rival be deposited at the next port and he returned with yet another string of pearls. Later, she said that women 'should never be jealous of a man's little needs, his little affairs. These affairs are not serious, and they don't touch real love'. Women, on the other hand, had big needs. 'It doesn't make them superior', Chanel said, 'but it does make them different'. When the Duke asked her once if she had been faithful to him while they were separated, she said that she had danced with a few men, but 'when they seemed to be leading further, [she] stopped dancing'.[17]

It may be that the Duke's ardour cooled, as it did in his relationships with other women; he may have realized that he could not marry her for two reasons: her class and her age. Unconventional and irreverent as he may have been, he surely had temptations within the British aristocracy. Moreover, Chanel was 46 years old when their affair ended and despite her consultations with doctors and midwives, despite the physical contortions she tried, she was not going to give him the son he desperately desired. She denied ever having told the Duke that she would not marry him because there had been many duchesses of Westminster but only one Chanel, a remark repeated in a great many articles about her; she maintained that she told him, in the face of his repeated proposals of marriage, that they did not need to be married since their affair was so delightful. Only if they had a child would she agree to marry him, she said. It is more likely that the Duke set out the bargain: only if she became pregnant would *he* consider marriage. His objective was an heir. He proposed to his third Duchess, the Honourable Loelia Ponsonby, after a courtship of three weeks. Her father, Sir Frederick Ponsonby (who became Baron Sysonby), was an intimate of the royal court: Treasurer to the King, Keeper of the Privy Purse and Lieutenant-Governor of Windsor Castle. Sir Frederick's younger brother, Arthur, was the leader of the Labour Party. Other than her pedigree, Loelia had age on her side: she was 27, more than two decades younger than he, when they married in February 1930.

Chanel apparently met Loelia when she and her mother were in Paris shopping for her trousseau, a meeting that Loelia found awkward because Chanel treated her like a child. The Duke was in Paris, too, and it is likely that he saw Chanel privately. She had no scruples about continuing an affair after a lover had married – rumour had it that 'Boy' Capel was on his way to meet her when his car crashed – but the Duke seemed to have lost interest.

Even without the Duke in residence, La Pausa became a central place for her social life. She held court there as if it were a palace and she, perhaps, a duchess. One guest, writer Roderick Cameron, recalled that he spent most of his visit listening to Chanel, because by that time Chanel rarely stopped talking. Something happened to Chanel after she lost Reverdy. The personality she revealed at work – overbearing, arrogant, dismissive, cruel – emerged as dominant in her social life too. 'Her moments of pensive silence disappeared', Pierre Galante noted. 'She became aggressive in her speech, talking, chattering and scoffing. Her behavior toward her friends changed.' She criticized, attacked, gossiped about one behind the backs of others. Anything, it seemed, 'was preferable to silence, so Coco talked'.[18] She talked to fill the emptiness of her life, to prevent herself from being overwhelmed by memories and regret, to insist on the importance of her own presence.

'I have known three people who talked to themselves, did not listen to your replies, and considered you on principle as an idiot: Claudel, Colette, and Chanel', Paul Morand recalled; 'whether the topic was the weaning of cats, eggs à la bourguignonne, a seam, or God, they explained to you that you didn't understand the first thing about it'.[19] Chanel once tried to explain herself: 'If my friends tease me for talking non-stop', she told Claude Delay, 'it's because they don't realise I'm terrified at the thought of being bored by other people. If I ever die I'm sure it will be of boredom.'[20]

So she talked and she talked. When she allowed someone else to enter the conversation, she hardly listened, but what she did hear, friends noticed, was to be later used against them. She had no scruples in betraying confidences and no trouble eliciting them with charming, apparently sincere, sympathy. 'It was a painful feeling', one of her lawyers remembered; 'one would have liked so much to be her friend ... Sometimes, I let myself be taken in. Each time, six months, nine months, one year later, what I had imprudently confided to her came back to me either as cannon-ball or as grapeshot.'[21]

'I remember her at La Pausa sitting on the floor of her terrace hugging her knees', Cameron recalled.

Our conversation escapes me, but not her presence, which was tomboyish but alluringly feminine – the nose slightly tilted, the eyes dark and lively, and the mouth mobile and curled up at the corners. With the years the eyes were to grow more and more simian.

She dressed as if for a performance, casual but strikingly chic, in slacks, a sweater and masses of jewellery: bracelets, pearl necklaces and precious stones. Cameron especially noticed a Maltese cross of rubies and 'blobs of emeralds'. At a time when servants were generally in attendance at meals, Chanel innovated the buffet, where guests chose among food in chafing dishes and platters. 'It made her nervous having servants around all the time, so banishing the footmen to the pantry she made us fend for ourselves, an unusual procedure in the Thirties, particularly in that kind of a house', Cameron remembered.[22]

La Pausa was precisely the kind of luxurious setting featured in fashion illustrations, where tall, slim women were shown in designer clothes at resorts, at Longchamp, dining in gardens or under the stars. Often, captions for illustrations indicated the names of the society women, as well as the designer who dressed them. 'Miss Elsie de Wolfe wears white chiffon embroidered in silver and broadly sashed with silver cloth', described a sketch of a Cheruit frock in *Vogue* (1 August 1918). In 1924, two women dressed in Chanel are shown standing in front of Coromandel screens. By 1926, though, while the settings in fashion illustrations became more detailed, women's faces became indistinguishable from one another. In French *Vogue* (1 June 1927), for example, a party at the races included La Comtesse de Breteuil and Lady Davies, both dressed in Chanel. Unlike earlier illustrations, however, which showed women's expressions (even if those expressions were demure, or bored), these faces were merely suggested – a line for a nose and a dark slash indicating lips.

This effacement also emerged in newly manufactured store mannequins, notably at the spectacular 1925 Paris Exposition promoting decorative arts. The Pavillon d'Élégance featured mannequins that exaggerated the height and slenderness of a woman's body. Tall, with elongated arms and legs, most startlingly of all they lacked facial features. This odd – and fleeting – change in representation preceded a noticeable change in styles: women who wore their hair short or shingled suddenly, by 1927, began to grow it long again. Parisian designers, Chanel foremost among them, led the new trend. Hemlines became longer, waists returned, skirts flared. By 1929, fashion reporters noted, the boyish look of the decade was gone.

Chanel took several steps to diversify in the late 1920s. In 1927 when she was still involved with Bendor, she opened a shop in London, hiring British models for her showings and British seamstresses to work under the supervision of a French *première*. Her costume jewellery became widely popular, and just as department stores and small shops in America stocked copies of Chanel clothing, these venues carried reproductions of the necklaces, bracelets and brooches that Chanel sold in Paris.

The Depression that began in America with the stock market crash in October 1929 did not make an impact in France until 1931. Despite the economic straits abroad, an atmosphere of revelry pervaded Paris, with what *New Yorker* correspondent Janet Flanner described as 'the greatest fancy-dress-ball season of all years'. Masquerades were especially popular, enabling Chanel to do a 'land-office business' dressing young men to appear as well-known socialites. Elsa Maxwell, Mrs Reginald Fellowes, the Duchess of Clermont-Tonnerre, and one or another of the Rothschilds, were hosts to these glittering gatherings.

Chanel threw her own glamorous parties, notably a summer gathering in July 1931 that garnered a headline in the *New York Times*: 'Chanel Entertains at Brilliant Fete.' 'Mlle Chanel's parties are known for their superb decorations and profusion of artistic talent', the article reported, describing the lavish al fresco affair, under a tent of gold tissue, illuminated with specially made projectors and festooned with white hydrangeas, lilacs and lilies. The guest list was fabulous: Consuelo Vanderbilt (at that time Mme Jacques Balsan); Joseph Widener and his son Peter; the Duchess of Alba; the Hon. Reginald Fellowes and his wife; Elsie de Wolfe (at that time Lady Mendel); Gloria Swanson (who was in Paris for fittings); the Grand-Duke Dmitri and his wife Audrey; Philippe Berthelot and his wife; Paul Morand and his wife; Baron Eugene de Rothschild and his wife; and other of the city's most well-known socialites. If any designers attended, the newspaper did not bother to list them.[23] This guest list was not unusual for Chanel; nor was it unusual for her to appear at parties hosted by princes, princesses and ambassadors. In December of the same year, she attended a reception for Prince Christopher of Greece, to which celebrities 'from many walks of Parisian and cosmopolitan life' took tea at the Théâtre des Champs-Elysées. Again, as reported in the *Times*, Chanel was the only couturière attending.[24]

The revelry was short-lived, however, and when the Depression hit France it lasted until 1936. Chanel's designs for 1931 reflect a new austerity – with cotton substituting for silk in both her Paris and London collections, and with zips in place of buttons. *Women's Wear Daily* reported on 4 February 1932 that Chanel announced drastic cuts in prices, and also that sketchers were banned from openings to prevent cheap copies. In addition to her fashion house and perfumes, however, Chanel wanted to take up a new opportunity to gain prestige and – she hoped – wealth: she would go to Hollywood.

6

Diva

Mademoiselle Chanel is a little black bull.

Colette, 1930 [1]

Chanel was approaching 50 in the early 1930s, as were many of her customers, and her fashions were no longer described as young but instead as 'smart' and, in response to the unsettled economy, 'practical'. *Time* magazine reported her to be one of the richest women in France, worth some $15 million (£9 million). [2] But a changing fashion world threatened her supremacy. Suddenly, her competitors were not Poiret and Vionnet – whose aesthetics she could predict – but a daring Italian, Elsa Schiaparelli, seven years younger than Chanel and even more flamboyant. Her bright colours and bold designs, some inspired by Dalí and Cocteau, seemed as fresh by the 1930s as Chanel's had seemed just after the First World War. Dismayed, Chanel discovered that some of her own customers had been lured to Schiaparelli's showrooms: first in a small garret at 4 rue de la Paix and after 1935 on the prestigious Place Vendôme, becoming Chanel's neighbour. And what's more, Schiaparelli was attractive, appeared at arts events and the best parties, and was photographed in glamorous company. In more ways than design, she was a threat to Chanel's place at the pinnacle of French fashion.

Like Chanel, Schiaparelli had begun her career with no experience in dressmaking, but with courage and imagination. Her aesthetic sense was far different from Chanel's: clothes, she said, should be 'architectural', built around the frame of a woman's body. 'The vagaries of lines and details or any asymmetric effect must always have a close connection with the frame', she said. 'The more the body is respected, the better the dress acquires vitality.' She noticed, of course, that the popular style of the time (which was initiated by Chanel) obliterated waists and compressed busts, two gestures that she rejected.

> Up with the shoulders!
> Bring the bust back into its own, pad the shoulders and
>   stop the ugly slouch!
> Raise the waist to its forgotten original place!
> Lengthen the skirt![3]

These became Schiaparelli's commands as she worked to carve her niche in Parisian *haute couture*. Soon, she became the talk of the city – and her reputation spread to America and American department store buyers. Like Chanel, she understood that copying afforded her free publicity, and she was delighted when department store advertisements featured clothing attributed to her style. Like Chanel, also, she celebrated her association with artists, whose designs she incorporated into her fanciful sweaters and hats.

Throughout 1929, to cite just one year of fashion reporting, Schiaparelli's status in the fashion world was rising. In February, the *New York Times* noticed the prevalence of ensembles in major collections, including Chanel's and Schiaparelli's. In spring, the newspaper reported similar colour palettes and designs in the collections of Lanvin, Chanel and Schiaparelli, all using tweeds and vivid solids; and Schiaparelli's bright blouses were singled out for notice at Biarritz. By the autumn of that year, the newspaper looked to Schiaparelli as an oracle of French fashion, reporting on her three-week visit to America, where she presented her sportswear featuring higher waistlines and skirt lengths of 10–15 cm (4–6 in.) below the knee. Her collection included outfits for aviation (linen, black patent leather and a zip), golf (in a soft shade of green), the beach (a swimsuit of shorts with a tucked-in orange blouse) and skiing (black gabardine covering a vivid coloured jumper). A bright red raincoat was made of rubberized silk and wool, with Schiaparelli's signature zip.[4]

Jean Cocteau extolled Schiaparelli as a designer who understood women's desires to dress with insouciance and individuality. In his customary hyperbole about fashion, he proclaimed that Schiaparelli could 'invent for all women – for each woman in particular – that violence which was once the privilege of the very few, of those who might be called the actresses in this drama-outside-theatre which is the World'. As the 'dressmaker of eccentricity', she had established in her shop in the Place Vendôme 'a devil's laboratory'.[5]

Schiaparelli's successful visit to America may have been one reason that Chanel embarked on her own journey there in February 1931, bound for California at the invitation of Samuel Goldwyn. Realizing that her costumes for Cocteau and Diaghilev had brought her positive publicity, she believed that exposure in films would enhance her reputation with a vast new audience. Other designers had worked on film wardrobes: Jeanne Lanvin for Abel Gance's *Napoléon* (1927); Jean Patou dressed Louise Brooks as Lulu in G. W. Pabst's *Pandora's Box* in 1929; and Paul Poiret worked on twelve French films. But American actresses were increasingly seen as trendsetters: Gloria Swanson, Ina Claire, Norma Talmadge – these film stars would now be free mannequins for Chanel. Another reason for the expedition may have been more personal: the need to strike out on a new path just a year after Bendor married Loelia Ponsonby. Once again, Chanel was alone. Once again, she turned to Misia, who accompanied her on board the ss *Europe* bound for New York, her first stop *en route* to Hollywood. Of course, a third reason was money. As George Bernard Shaw once remarked about his own conversation with Sam Goldwyn, they 'had no trouble understanding each other. He talked art and I talked money.'[6] It's likely that Chanel could have said the same. Goldwyn apparently offered her one million dollars.

Chanel's journey was big news. Reporters crowded into her suite at the Hotel Pierre in Manhattan after she arrived there on 4 March. Through an interpreter, she told them that she had signed no contract with Goldwyn but had agreed to meet film stars and get a sense of what a commitment might entail. She confessed that she herself rarely went to the cinema in Paris, but in one movie that she did remember, which was set in the frozen North, the star wore an open-backed evening gown. She promised that no one would see such nonsense from her designs. It was not movies, however, that reporters wanted to talk about. Instead, they wanted to take note of what she wore (a red jersey outfit with white piqué collar and cuffs); what she thought about pyjamas as evening wear ('I detest them', she announced); and what she thought about men's perfumes ('Disgusting!').[7]

'This is the first time a *couturière* of such importance, or indeed any, has left the native heath', Janet Flanner wrote in the *New Yorker*, ignoring the previous visit of Chanel's competitor Schiaparelli.

> Considering what universal style-setting means to Paris for the maintenance of its financial and artistic pulse, the departure of Chanel for California must be more important than that of Van Dyck for the English Court of Charles I.[8]

The departure was postponed, though, when Chanel came down with influenza, forcing her to recuperate at Pierre for eleven days. Finally, she was well enough to board a transcontinental train, heading west.

Goldwyn treated Chanel like his personal treasure, showing her off to Hollywood royalty – including Greta Garbo, Marlene Dietrich,

Katharine Hepburn and Claudette Colbert. Introducing her as 'the biggest fashion brain ever known', he ensconced her on the set of his new production, the comedy *Palmy Days* starring Eddie Cantor. Her second project was to be *Tonight or Never*, featuring Gloria Swanson. Goldwyn had no ideas of his own about costumes; he was interested only in allying himself with Chanel's reputation, and Chanel was interested, likewise, in what he could do for her. How she was to work remains unknown. Goldwyn expected her to make two visits a year as fashion adviser, not working on site, but instead getting a sense of the actresses' needs for particular roles. She claimed that she was going to return to Paris with wardrobe ideas and then send these ideas to Hollywood. In Paris, she said: 'I will create and design gowns six months ahead for the actresses in Mr Goldwyn's pictures. I will send the sketches from Paris and my fitters in Hollywood will make the gowns.' But it is a mystery how a designer who worked on models and did not draw was going to transmit these ideas, and the process was contradicted months later when Gloria Swanson arrived at rue Cambon for fittings.

Chanel spent two weeks in Hollywood and then another week in New York, where she was fêted by Carmel Snow (editor of *Harper's Bazaar*) and the venerable publisher Condé Nast, whose relationship with Chanel – always rocky – became warmer. On Easter Sunday, wearing a beige suit and matching hat, Chanel strolled with some friends in the Easter Parade on Fifth Avenue; she was delighted, she said, by the women's chic holiday clothes and the fresh flowers that adorned their outfits. She was also occupied with hiring new models: twenty American women sailed home with her when she left on 10 April, this time on the French liner *Paris*.

According to Axel Madsen, Chanel returned to Hollywood during the summer, designing the wardrobe for *The Greeks Had a Word for Them* with Ina Claire and Joan Blondell, but she was not satisfied with her association with Goldwyn and her outfits for the stars did not garner the kind of publicity she may have wanted. Her simple designs and conservative colours translated on film as somewhat staid and dowdy. Although an article in the *Washington Post* maintained that Hollywood was the new style centre for American women, Chanel was rarely singled out for mention in film reviews.[9] Hollywood, she found, was a world she could not dominate.

Paris, however, was. According to photographer Horst P. Horst, Chanel was the centre of social life in the 1930s when he arrived in Paris at the age of 24. He soon took a job as an apprentice to the architect Le Corbusier and was drawn into an artistic circle that included several photographers who worked for *Vogue*. Through Janet Flanner, he was invited to go to New York for six months to work for Condé Nast as a fashion photographer. There, he found that possibilities for originality were more circumscribed than in Paris. There were no model agencies, for example, and models were invited because they were known by some of the Condé Nast staff who thought they might photograph well. Many were friends, or daughters of friends, of Nast. How and where they could be photographed conformed strictly to convention: stiff poses against a monochrome background, highlighting details of the clothing. Horst returned to Paris before the six months had elapsed and began to work for French *Vogue*.

His reputation quickly grew and he became part of Chanel's world. He photographed Natalie Paley (who modelled for her husband, Lucien Lelong) and through her he met Marie-Laure de Noailles, Fulco di Verdura (who was designing jewellery for Chanel) and Cocteau. He got to know Schiaparelli before Chanel, photographing her in a 'blackamoor' costume for the Bal Oriental in 1934. 'For six or seven years', Horst said, 'she was more talked about than anyone else in the Paris couture world . . . Schiap went all out to be noticed. The high-heeled shoe that she designed for use as a hat was a typical Schiaparelli invention. Heaven knows who actually wore it . . . but it made news, and that was what she was after.'[10]

A craze for costume balls kept designers busy in the 1930s as they had to make outfits for those who attended, as well as appear at the balls themselves. Chanel 'blacked up' for her appearance at the Fête Coloniale in 1931; as the artist Berthe Morisot at the Bal des Copies de Tableaux; as a gypsy at the Bal Oriental in 1935; as a tree at the Bal de la Forêt in 1938; and as Jean-Antoine Watteau's painting *Indifferent* at the Bal du Tricentenaire de Racine in 1939. In the spring of 1934, Horst went to the Bal des Valses, held on an island in the lake of the Bois de Boulogne and hosted by the famed party-giver Baron Nicolas de Gunzburg. The ball was de Gunzburg's fabulous, opulent, farewell gesture to his native city before he sailed permanently to America. Guests were invited to dress as historical figures associated with the late nineteenth-century Imperial Habsburg court in Vienna. A selection of guests most imaginatively attired was asked to come to the *Vogue* studios to be photographed by Horst in their costumes. At two in the morning, the ball barely winding down, Horst himself was photographed with Chanel, the first time he had seen her. She was dressed as Queen Victoria in mourning, in an elaborate hoop-skirted black taffeta gown.

In Paris, she was among the most photographed women of the time. Horst, Man Ray, Baron Adolph de Meyer, George Hoyningen-Huene and Cecil Beaton all made iconic portraits of Chanel, dressed in black, with her pearls and her cigarette. In 1937, a photograph by Francois Kollar dominated an advertisement for Chanel No. 5, her best-known creation. Kollar showed Chanel standing in front of the fireplace in her apartment at the Ritz, wearing an elegant black gown, black ankle-strap heels and pearls. 'Madame Gabrielle Chanel is above all an artist in living', the advertisement proclaimed. 'Her dresses, her perfumes, are created with a faultless instinct for drama. Her Perfume No. 5 is like the soft music that underlies the playing of a love scene. It kindles the imagination; indelibly fixes the scene in the memories of the players.'

Chanel, photographed by Cecil Beaton, 1937.

Chanel in her suite at the Ritz, photographed by François Kollar, 1937.

Chanel was an artist in living and, according to Horst, an artist in orchestrating the drama of her social life. 'She was omnipresent and omnipotent', he recalled.

She argued and pontificated; she set up an alarm clock on her table when Dali was present, and insisted that after he had spoken for ten minutes without interruption, she had the right to do the same. Often she would be molding jewel settings in putty between her fingers as she talked. Costume jewelry was only one of her many inventions.[11]

In 1932, however, Chanel decided to turn from paste to precious stones, opening her home in the Faubourg Saint-Honoré for an exhibition of diamonds, with the proceeds to go to charity. The designs, as Janet Flanner described them in the *New Yorker*, were

delicately astronomical. Magnificent lopsided stars for earrings; as a necklace, a superb comet whose nape-encircling tail is all that attaches it to a lady's throat; bracelets that are flexible rays; crescents for hats and hair; and, as a unique set piece mounted in yellow gold, a splendid sun of yellow diamonds from a unique collection of matched stones unmatched in the world.

As Flanner noted, the exhibition which took place at the height of the Depression was just one more piece of evidence that Chanel had an 'aggravating instinct to strike when everyone else thinks the iron is cold'.[12]

The art of living, for Chanel, always included lovers. In 1932, she had an affair with 26-year-old Luchino Visconti. According to one of Visconti's biographers, Chanel had come to lunch at his family's residence (the Villa Erba in Cernobbio, near Lake Como) when Visconti was still a child, which apparently was during a trip she took in 1922 with Misia and José Sert. Visconti would have been sixteen. He saw her again in Venice where, along with Lifar, Misia and the Vicomtesse de Noailles, she visited the palazzo where his sisters-in-law, Madina and Niki, lived. And then in Paris he met her again through parties given by Madina and Niki.

Some who saw the pair together noticed that Visconti, although he spoke French fluently, was very shy with Chanel, whom he considered a 'great goddess of Paris society'. He often dined with her at the rue Cambon and spent time at La Pausa. Young, handsome, rich and attentive, Visconti met all of Chanel's requirements in a lover. Visconti, for his part, noted her volatility, her pride, her cattiness and her need to punish others – and herself.[13] Horst remembered that she 'bullied' Visconti into finding direction for his life; to give him a push, she introduced him to the film-maker Jean Renoir who was making *A Day in the Country* in 1935. This connection proved fateful for Visconti's career as a director – and for Chanel, as well: a few years later, she designed the wardrobe for Renoir's *The Rules of the Game* (1939).

What seemed to her like a last chance at love materialized in the person of artist, publisher, decorator and essayist Paul Iribe. Before the First World War, Iribe had published a weekly magazine, *Le Témoin* ('The Witness'), featuring his own illustrations and caricatures; and in 1914, with Jean Cocteau, he founded *Le Mot*, which despite its name ('The Word') was heavily and sumptuously illustrated. *Le Mot* folded after a year but Iribe had other outlets for his talents: he was a prominent fashion illustrator, notably working with Paul Poiret, for whom he produced a luxurious book, *Les Robes de Paul Poiret, racontées par Paul Iribe*. Poiret was enchanted, both by the book and by the mysterious, alluring Iribe himself. 'He was an extremely odd chap', Poiret recalled in his memoirs, 'a Basque plump as a capon, and reminding one both of a seminarist and of a printer's reader. In the seventeenth century he would have been a Court abbé.'[14]

A cloistered life, however, would never have interested Iribe. By all accounts an opportunist eager for status and especially money, in 1918 he divorced his first wife, actress Jeanne Diris, after seven years of marriage. His second wife more aptly fitted his needs: she was an American heiress, Maybelle Hogan. The couple lived in Hollywood after Iribe took a position as an artistic director for Paramount Pictures, but he clashed too often with his associates (one of whom was Cecil B. DeMille). By 1926 he was fired and returned to Paris with his wife and son. There, Maybelle backed his project to design and sell furniture, rugs, fabrics and jewellery at a shop on the rue Faubourg Saint-Honoré. Referred by Maybelle, Chanel gave him a commission to design jewellery for her. By the early 1930s the business arrangement had become an affair and when Maybelle discovered the betrayal she left him, taking their children (they had a daughter in 1928) to America.

As her friends could not help but notice, Chanel was obviously in love. She claimed later to have regretted her passion for Iribe. 'How I loathe passion! What an abomination, what a ghastly disease!' she exclaimed to Paul Morand.

> Passion is Lourdes on a daily basis . . . I had great affection for Paul and was very fond of him, but now that he is dead, and after such a long time, I can't help feeling irritated when I think of the atmosphere of passion he built around me. He wore me out, he ruined my health.[15]

In 1919, when Chanel was newly ascendant in the fashion world, Iribe had been more famous in Paris than she; but by the 1930s Chanel was the star and Iribe's reputation had fallen. His jealousy, she came to believe, made him sadistic. 'Iribe loved me, but he did so because of all those things that he never admitted to himself, nor admitted to me; he loved me with the secret hope of destroying me', she said. 'He longed for me to be crushed and humiliated . . .

It would have made him deeply happy to see me belong totally to him, impoverished, reduced to helplessness, paralysed and driving a small car.'[16] Yet passion raged and Chanel decided to take Iribe on as a business partner, bestowing upon him full power of attorney and allowing him to preside over a board meeting at Les Parfums Chanel, shocking the members who had assembled. Equally shocking to many who knew her was the rumour that she and Iribe planned to marry. 'That such an independent-spirited woman as Mlle. Chanel should marry has caused considerable surprise among her friends', reported the *New York Times*, 'but then, they say, "One can never be quite sure what Coco will do next"'. Another surprise disclosed in the article was that she planned to move from her house at Faubourg Saint-Honoré to a more modest home, 'devoting a large part of her fortune to charity work'.[17] Clearly, moving to a more modest house was Iribe's idea. He criticized her for not being simple, she said. 'What's the point of all these objects?' he admonished her. 'Your way of life is ruining you . . . Why do you need all these servants? . . . I'd come here more often, I might live close to you, if you knew how to be happy with nothing.'[18] She found two rooms near her home where she installed herself with a few necessities: some favourite books, some precious rugs. Is this how you want to live, she asked him? As she guessed, Iribe was repulsed at the idea and soon she reinstalled herself at the Ritz where he took rooms opposite. Iribe, she said, was 'the most complicated man [she] ever knew'.[19]

His own complications reveal some of Chanel's. Iribe was xenophobic, anti-Semitic, a radical nationalist and reactionary. He applauded Fascism and admired the order and discipline trumpeted by Nazi Germany. When Chanel underwrote the republication of *Le Témoin* in 1933, Iribe's right-wing views were displayed in full view – and so was Chanel, whom Iribe depicted in a drawing as the embodiment of France: fallen, wounded, languishing. Nevertheless, Chanel adored him and she believed that at last, at the age of 50, she had found a companion for the rest of her life.

Chanel, photographed by Adolphe de Meyer, 1936.

Then, one September morning in 1935, they were playing tennis at Roquebrune when she approached the net to tell Iribe not to hit so hard; he glanced at her over his glasses and collapsed. He had suffered a massive heart attack. Guilty that she had pressed him to play that morning, and overcome with grief, she broke down. 'She couldn't sleep any more', Claude Delay said. 'Sedol was her last defense against night – the ultimate and solitary penetration.'[20]

Again she turned to work, where she had always been able to exert control; but in 1936 that world was threatened. If Chanel explained her success by luck, then her luck changed when Léon Blum's Socialist Popular Front took control of the French government, inspiring an economic revolution. Throughout the country, workers struck for such guarantees as an eight-hour day and paid vacations. Her own workers joined the strikes: 150 of them occupied the atelier, stopping production and sales, demanding higher wages and a weekly salary, rather than payment for piece work. She refused, telling them that with economic conditions so bad she could not fulfil the kind of contract they demanded. Instead, according to a front-page report in the *New York Times*, she offered them the business. They could run it themselves, she said, at their own risk, and she would serve as an unpaid consultant. If they turned down her offer, she had no choice but to close down, permanently. For the workers to accept, though, they would have needed to come up with enough capital to take over the fashion house – an unlikely prospect.[21]

Not interested in the offer, the workers pressed her to meet with them. Stubbornly, she continued to refuse; but in mid-June, her lawyer, René de Chambrun, advised her that she must meet with delegates if she had any hope of saving her business. Finally on 30 June she agreed to negotiate. After she conceded to some of their demands, the workers left and Chanel reopened on 1 July. On 26 July, the *New York Times* ran a small advertisement, bordered in black, dateline Paris: 'To put a stop to unpleasant rumours – MADEMOISELLE CHANEL announces that she will show her Winter Collection on August 5.' She would go on but her workers' defiance, which she saw as flagrant betrayal, left her wounded.

Chanel in Venice, 1936.

7

History

The day that a woman has no more courage, that's old age.

Chanel, 1937[1]

A new silhouette characterized fashions by the late 1930s: small waists and full skirts. Ruffles, flowers, lace – all these features signified the end of the slim, unadorned styles that had made Chanel's reputation the decade before. Like other designers, Chanel embraced the change, offering dresses with 'nipped-in' waists and flounces, cotton piqué blouses resembling shirts, fanciful jewelled buttons and bows; no one, fashion reporters commented, handled lace with Chanel's delicacy. She started being described as 'a champion of all that is feminine in dress'.[2]

Not surprisingly, women tried to shape their bodies to fit the new styles. 'Slimming menus' made their way into newspapers and magazines, advising women to consume around 1,100 calories a day and practise bending exercises to achieve a 'champagne glass' figure. The hourglass figure was gone and forgotten. *Vogue* showed a photograph of a model wearing a body mask, which hardened and supposedly removed fat as it was washed off. Manufacturers offered special corsets: in an advertisement for the 'All-in-One', the undergarment company Lily of France asked: 'Do you want to wear Vionnet's Grecian uplift line, Chanel's trim waistline, Patou's suave hipline? Then let this Lily of France rayon brocade all-in-one "line you up" with Paris spring fashions.'[3]

In April 1937, a month before fashion leaders showed their creations at the long-awaited Paris International Exposition des Arts et Techniques, dresses became especially romantic. Fashion reporters noted that the line was sylph-like, the waist cinched and skirts more voluminous than ever – up to 27–37 m (88–121 ft) of fabric. Chanel was one of several designers who emphasized the underskirt, 'contrasting it in colour to that of the floating overskirt that undulates in swaying rhythm as one walks', as *New York Times* fashion editor Virginia Pope described it.[4]

The established elite of couture were still Chanel's rivals: other than Schiaparelli (whose wide-shouldered styles emphasized tiny waistlines), Mainbocher, Molyneux, Lanvin, Patou, Vionnet and Worth dominated Paris fashion. But a growing cadre of young designers, all under 40, now emerged on the scene, among them Maggy Rouff (whose simplicity and refinement echoed Chanel's designs), Jacques Heim (an innovator in furs and bathing suits), Charles Creed (heir to a 200-year-old fashion house, famous for his elegantly tailored suits), Marcel Rochas (especially admired for his sportswear) and Alix Grès (founder of the House of Alix, whose talent at draping evoked Vionnet, and whose designing technique – directly on a model – and preference for soft jerseys evoked Chanel). For the winter collection, shown in August 1937, Alix and Chanel were linked in a *New York Times* headline as leaders of the season's styles, with twelve paragraphs of the article extolling Alix's designs as 'fascinating', 'a sensation' and 'a miracle', to ten paragraphs describing Chanel as 'charming' and 'full of a new and fresh spirit'.[5] Except for competition from other French designers, Chanel was also aware that the American fashion world was flowering. Virginia Pope heralded this development with patriotic pride, and her reports in the *New York Times* throughout the 1930s and '40s triumphantly noted the rise of young designers whose 'indescribable but unmistakable' talent was uniquely American.[6] None of Chanel's young competitors, though, had yet become a celebrity. For example, although Alix was petite and charming, she was also modest and shy, and when not at work, she stayed at home with her daughter.

Chanel, on the other hand, stayed in the news: in Monte Carlo; at the Lido in Venice; at a dinner with Serge Lifar, Marie-Laure de Noailles, Igor Stravinsky and his mistress Vera Soudeikine. She invited French *Vogue* to do a spread on her villa at La Pausa where she was photographed climbing a tree, posing on a staircase, and – wearing a satin bed jacket – propped against pillows in her bedroom. She appeared in *Vogue* with Lifar, dressed in chic white slacks and a turban; drawings in *Harper's Bazaar* show her riding a donkey at Capri (where she was vacationing with Misia), drinking Americanos and dancing at the Quisisana.[7] In June 1938, she appeared in *Vogue* at a meal given by the Prince and Princess de Faucigny-Lucinge at Hotel de Paris in Monte Carlo, where other guests included Grand-Duke Dmitri, Christian Bérard, Dalí, Count Étienne de Beaumont and Boris Kochno.

Chanel was the first woman pictured in an advertisement for Chanel No. 5, exuding glamour; and she was memorably photographed by Horst, whose prestige in the fashion world was rising as he became known as an innovator. Although exposure time for film was very slow – two or three seconds – which made it impossible for models to show emotion, Horst strived to reveal personality and he was one of the few photographers to use sets. He devised lighting that made it possible to photograph black clothing without washing out a woman's complexion. After the Depression, when *Vogue* and *Vanity Fair* were struggling to survive, Condé Nast often turned to Horst to generate interest in the magazines. Judging from Chanel's willingness to be photographed by Horst, it appears that she too admired his work.

Her chance to sit for him came in the summer of 1937 when Horst joined Bettina Wilson (later, Ballard), American *Vogue*'s fashion editor, for dinner at an elegant restaurant in the Romanian pavilion of the Paris International Exposition. Chanel and Misia were also

Chanel with Serge Lifar in a photograph by Jean Moral, 1937.

dining there with a friend, the Egyptian man-about-town Félix Rollo, whom Horst knew, and Rollo invited Horst and Bettina to join their table. Rollo and his party soon finished their meal and left but Horst had been seen dining with them, news that quickly reached French *Vogue*. Would Chanel agree to be photographed by Horst, wearing her own dress, the editors asked?

She arrived at the studio with an assistant and a white lace dress. When Horst sent proofs to her, she admitted that Horst had done well by her dress but not by her. 'How could I possibly take a good portrait of you?' he replied, 'I hardly know you.' So a few days later, Chanel invited him to dinner in her apartment at the Ritz, along with their mutual friend Solange d'Ayen, fashion editor of French *Vogue*. The apartment seemed huge to Horst during that first visit, although he later realized that it was quite small. The expensive and well-chosen furnishings included a *chaise-longue* near the fireplace and the famous Coromandel lacquer screens. Dinner – brought up from the hotel – was served by waiters. Chanel, 'in rather savage fun', proceeded to tear apart the Schiaparelli suit that Solange was wearing, to show how badly it was made. Solange took this calmly but Horst felt both intimidated and entranced.

The next week, Chanel came again to *Vogue*'s studio, this time to be photographed for herself. Again she brought an assistant who carried her bags and jewellery. For this session, though, she wore black. Horst remembered that Bettina Wilson stayed in the studio to watch, fiddling with some of the jewellery that Horst had laid out for Chanel's selection. Exasperated, Chanel told her she could take one of the necklaces 'on one condition: that you leave us alone'.[8] This sitting was much more successful than the first one: a series of photographs of Chanel show her reclining on a *chaise-longue*, in black dress, with a ribbon in her hair and a cigarette between her fingers; and another, again in black, with a jewelled hat, looking defiantly into the camera.[9] She loved the portraits, ordered many copies, and requested a bill. When

Chanel, photographed by Horst, 1937.

Horst responded with a note declaring it an honour to have
photographed her, Chanel came back with another request:
to be invited to dinner with Misia at rue Saint-Romain where
Horst lived.

They came to his apartment resplendent in gowns and floor-
length black mink coats, and dined on veal, served by Horst's butler
on a card table in front of the fireplace; the apartment, Chanel
noticed, was sparsely and simply furnished. The two women talked
mostly with one another, and Horst thought they were 'rather
intrigued by their little adventure'. Chanel seemed to take pleasure
in showing him off to Misia, and it was clear to him that she did not

want him to become friends with her. Years later, when he saw Misia for the last time, she told him: 'That wicked Coco, she never allowed you and me to get to know one another.'[10]

The morning after the dinner, Chanel summoned Horst to rue Cambon, where he followed her up to the attic filled with furniture and objects that had once been in her house at Faubourg Saint-Honoré. He admired one beautiful piece and another, unaware of Chanel's reputation for impulsive largesse. The next day, a van pulled up to his apartment and delivered all of the chairs, consoles and mirrors that he had praised. The furniture seemed far too sumptuous for his Paris apartment so he soon shipped it to his Sutton Place apartment overlooking the East River in Manhattan.[11]

As part of Chanel's circle, Horst observed that she used social occasions to perform and one of the most polished acts in her repertoire was seduction. She was forthright about her attraction to him – and to others – even if she knew that a man's sexual preference was for other men. She frequently invited Horst to accompany her to various events, such as going to the opera, a dress rehearsal of Cocteau's *Les Chevaliers de la Table Ronde* or a new theatre production. Being seen with younger men – Horst, for example, who was more than two decades younger than Chanel – made her feel attractive and desirable.

At 54 years old, Chanel shared her secrets of youthfulness in a new fashion magazine, *Marie Claire*. 'Oh, youth! How can you preserve it?' she asked. By having confidence, she claimed, by arming oneself with courage, keeping one's heart and spirit alive: above all, by being natural. A youthful spirit, she said, will emanate from one's face; an inner beauty will make a woman beautiful physically. One must never complain, 'I'm no longer young' or pretend to have a false innocence. To age well, one must know how to live well. The women that men love – as companions, as lovers, as wives – are those who can ease a man's life and smooth away difficulties. After the age of 40, she said, a woman is responsible for her own expression. One wrinkle more or less, what does it matter? What matters is elegance, in morale above all – that is the true youthfulness, of the spirit and the heart.[12]

What mattered to Chanel was being admired and after Iribe died her name was linked to several men. The Spanish sculptor Apel.les Fenosa was one of these men. In 1939, after he returned to Paris from his native Spain, he fashioned a head of Chanel and they apparently became lovers. According to Axel Madsen, she fell in love – briefly – with Harrison Williams, a wealthy American whose wife (a fashion model) was a friend of the newly married Duchess of Windsor. Chanel's impetuous flirtations continued until her death. Publisher and reputed womanizer Guy Schoeller (whose most famous wife was Françoise Sagan) admitted that in the 1960s, after driving Chanel home in his Mercedes Papillon from a dinner with Hélène and Pierre Lazareff (she the founder of *Elle* and he of *France-Soir*) Chanel, smitten by his charms, asked him to marry her. James Brady, Paris bureau chief for *Women's Wear Daily*, in his early thirties when he met Chanel in 1961, called himself 'her last amour'. She was nearly aged 80 when she developed an infatuation with him. Women friends remember that when a man entered a room she lit up, no matter who he was, no matter what her age. Seduction was a reflex.

Professionally, she seemed restless. Although her showings continued on schedule and the fashion world looked to her for elegance, she knew she was not perceived as the rebel, the innovator and the leader as she had been a decade before. *Haute couture* clients were diminishing and the United States government did not help by initiating a crackdown on non-criminal smuggling: that is, on men and women who brought in luxury items from Europe without declaring their value and paying duties. Clients of fashion designers had long been cutting labels out of their purchases, hiding them in their luggage and having their maids re-sew them at home. Now, the government was intent on prosecuting these offenders, fining them and even sentencing them to prison. Elma N. Lauer, the wife of New York Supreme Court Justice Edgar J. Lauer, pleaded guilty to charges in December 1938 after police raided her Park Avenue apartment. Included in the indictment were dresses by Chanel, Schiaparelli and other noted designers. The comedians George Burns and Jack Benny were accused of smuggling jewellery; and in May 1939, customs agents – specially trained to identify *haute couture* gowns, even if they lacked a label – enacted a three-hour search in the penthouse of one Mrs James C. Ayer at the Upper East Side of Manhattan. They found 37 items, purchased on three separate European trips, including several by Chanel. Of £4,500 worth of dresses and furs brought back in 1935, for example, Ayer had only declared £450.

Chanel complained about customers who bought only one or two outfits, and who flitted from one designer to another. Her favourite clients in the 1930s were American socialites Laura Corrigan – the fabulously wealthy widow of Cleveland steel magnate James Corrigan – and Barbara Hutton – the Woolworth heiress, who bought some 30 outfits when she attended wedding festivities for the Duke of Windsor and Wallis Simpson. The often-wed Hutton had been married to Alexis Mdivani, the brother of Roussy Sert, until the couple parted in 1935. Chanel could count on Hutton and Corrigan to order dozens of outfits at a time; and she could also count on Roussy, who was profiled in *Harper's Bazaar* claiming that all her clothing – and sense of style – must be attributed to Chanel.

In the winter of 1938 Chanel was in Lausanne when once again she became involved with the Serts' complicated lives. Alex-Ceslas Rzewuski – a Dominican friar and confidant of Misia – was in Freiburg when Misia called him from Lourdes on the afternoon of 15 December, desperately seeking help for Roussy, whose health had deteriorated soon after she and Sert returned home from a cruise. Doctors in Lausanne, where the couple then were, first attributed the precipitous decline to her increasing daily doses of morphine and they insisted that she be admitted immediately to a clinic in Prangins for detoxification. Within hours, however, Sert himself called Rzewuski saying that it was not drug addiction but advanced tuberculosis that was killing his wife. Although for months after their marriage Roussy had been losing weight and weakening, physicians that the couple consulted in Sweden, America and Paris had failed to take x-rays, instead proposing psychotherapy. Now, it seemed, Roussy was beyond help, with only hours to live.

Sert pleaded with Rzewuski to rush to his wife's bedside. When he arrived at the clinic, he found the distraught Sert together with Roussy's sister Nina and her husband Denys Conan Doyle (the son of Arthur Conan Doyle), the orchestra conductor Igor Markevitch and Chanel. But instead of welcoming the friar, the group barred the door to Roussy's room. The door was shut, Chanel told him, because they feared that if Roussy thought a priest had come to give her last rites, it would only hasten her death. Although Rzewuski argued that he could offer comfort to Roussy, his words had no effect. Chanel still stood firmly against the door, her arms crossed – in a gesture, Rzewuski recalled, worthy of Sarah Bernhardt. He could do nothing, he decided, but on his way out of the clinic he encountered a sympathetic nurse and begged to be let into Roussy's room. The nurse, a Catholic, understood the situation; since the guards outside the room had disbanded, Rzewuski managed to slip in.

Weak, thin, certain she was dying, Roussy asked him where he had been and called him close to her. They remained talking quietly until around eight or nine that evening. When Sert and the others returned, he told them that Roussy not only was calm but truly happy. This time with no argument from the others, he decided to stay in the clinic overnight. Around two in the morning, a knock on the door roused him and he rushed to Roussy's room, where he found the group standing around her bed in silence. Not 30 minutes later, Roussy died.

As the drama unfolded, Misia was bound for Lausanne from Lourdes, arriving after Roussy died. Like Rzewuski, she was rebuffed, told by the hotel doorman that she would not be allowed to pay her respects at Roussy's coffin, nor to attend the funeral planned for the next day. All doors were closed to her – on the orders of Sert or, Misia guessed, Chanel. Wounded by the affront, she left immediately for Paris.[13] For his part, Sert left for Madrid, where he took a lover – the wife of Germany's ambassador to Spain. But he soon fled war-torn Spain for Paris, and to Misia. Chanel once again became part of their intimate circle. Her relationship with Misia survived all trials, insults and jealousy.

War in Spain and rumours of war elsewhere in Europe darkened the atmosphere for the Paris fashion showings in early 1939. American buyers were eager to sail home, uncertain about when – or if – they would be returning. Hitler's invasion of Czechoslovakia (now divided between the Czech Republic and Slovakia) in March and Mussolini's invasion of Albania and Greece made the prospect of war imminent, however much newspapers reported hopes for a diplomatic solution. Fashion houses bravely tried to offer a distraction from the gnawing fear of conflict. Chanel's fashion showing in August 1939 was a triumph: coats, suits, gowns – all were opulent, with velvet, velour, tweeds, furs and especially heavy black satin recurring in several ensembles. Even the colours – rich red, bronze, earthy brown – were luxurious. Opulence characterized other showings too: Lanvin, Vionnet, Alix all seemed to rail, by sheer extravagance, against the inevitability of war.

Besides readying her opening, Chanel spent the summer of 1939 furiously designing costumes for Salvador Dalí's ballet *Bacchanale* for the Ballets Russes de Monte Carlo, choreographed by Léonide Massine. What Dalí called 'The First Paranoiac Ballet' was scheduled to open at New York's Metropolitan Opera House in November. He had worked on it during a four-month stay at La Pausa the year before, when he shared the house with another guest, Pierre

Reverdy. When Chanel – whom Dalí called his best friend – came to stay for a while, his happiness was complete. When she returned to Paris, Dalí kept up a frequent correspondence with 'belle petite Coco', as he addressed her in his letters. Among Dalí's other projects at La Pausa were his autobiography, *Secret Life*, and an ominous painting, *The Enigma of Hitler*, inspired, he said, by his dreams of war.

Frightening rumours became fact when France joined Britain in declaring war against Germany. By 2 September 1939, France had mobilized three million men, and the streets and cafés of Paris emptied. Cars, taxis and metro trains brought soldiers to railway stations throughout the city. Some carried knapsacks, and some tin helmets inherited from soldiers who fought in the last war. Women, children, elderly couples and pets jammed into taxis and headed out of the city, hoping to find a safe refuge. The American Committee for Devastated France (ACDF), disbanded after 1919, hastily came together again to facilitate evacuations. Those who stayed in Paris dug out their bicycles and slung gas masks over their shoulders. It was against the law to be on the street without one. Many shops and a third of the post offices closed for lack of workers.

Just before 4 a.m. on Tuesday 5 September, a siren shrieked throughout the city signalling the first air raid of the war. Men, women and children – most in night clothes and some carrying dogs and cats in their arms – proceeded calmly to shelters (there were several on every block, and one for every hotel). More than two hours later, when no bombs had fallen, they began to emerge slowly into the Paris morning, following milk trucks along their routes, some stopping for coffee on the way home. The tension of that day only increased as the city waited, day after day and month after month, for attack.

Some designers were called up for military service; others left the country. Schiaparelli went to America, Molyneux to England.

Chanel decided, suddenly and without notice to her workers, to shut down. Her employees thought she was taking revenge against their strike three years before, but Chanel denied it, claiming that she closed because she knew there would be no market for *haute couture*. Since she awoke from the previous war a famous designer, her decision seems more complicated: fatigue, irritability at the success of her competitors and the Wertheimers' business reorganization, which diminished her authority at Parfums Chanel – all these may have contributed to her closing down.

As the war went on – the 'phony' war, as the first months came to be known, because up to that point France had not been attacked – some designers who had been conscripted were allowed to return to work in an industry that the French government felt was vital for the country's future. Prominent among them was Lucien Lelong, president of the Chambre Syndicale de la Couture Parisienne, who was determined to keep couture alive in Paris. Even without foreign buyers in the city, even with dire restrictions on fabrics and supplies, he was certain that sales could continue. He begged Chanel to reconsider, but she stood firm. Like many other Parisians who feared bombings and dire shortages of food, electricity and even water, she decided to leave the city for the south of France soon after war was declared.

According to Dalí, Chanel appeared at the quiet seaside town of Arcachon, near Bordeaux and the Spanish border, where she joined him, Gala, Marcel Duchamp and the free-wheeling Surrealist painter Léonor Fini. They passed the time dining out together, but also intently listening for news on the radio. 'Coco was like a white swan', Dalí remembered, 'her thoughtful brow slightly bowed, moving forward on the water of history which was beginning to flood everything, with the unique elegance and grace of French intelligence'.[14] It is likely that Chanel was not as serene as Dalí remembered her, but she may have seemed calm compared to him. Apart from an overwhelming fear of war, Dalí was also filled with anxiety about his ballet which was scheduled to open in New York in less than two months. Chanel would not allow her costumes to travel from Europe unless Dalí himself accompanied them, but Gala refused even to think about the possibility: her husband should not risk a sea journey during war. There seemed no alternative but to find a quick substitute, and Dalí's New York representatives enlisted the designer Madame Karinska, who worked tirelessly to ready costumes in four days.

After the initial shock and fright, Paris gradually returned to life: theatres offered a few performances a week, restaurants and nightclubs (despite an early curfew) drew customers. The market at Les Halles, which formerly opened before daybreak, now operated only in the early afternoon, but food seemed surprisingly abundant. Booksellers took their places along the Seine, and although sandbags circled public buildings, these too reopened. With news from Paris portraying the city as quiet and calm, Chanel left Arcachon after two weeks and headed home.

As other fashion houses worked on their collections, Chanel stayed in her apartment at the Ritz, keeping up a social life with friends who remained in the city: Serge Lifar, Lady Mendl, Étienne de Beaumont, the Rothschilds, Armand de Gramont and many others. There were still private parties, and as the months went on restaurants and theatres drew their customary crowds. By winter, though, Chanel was frustrated by idleness. Shortly after New Year's Day, 1940, Horst received a letter from her, the only one she ever wrote to him. She claimed not to be seeing people, that she was tired and 'full of ideas for many things in the future. But at the moment one must keep still, and that's very difficult for me!'[15]

By early May, the war was drawing closer. Germany had swept over Belgium and crossed into France. Paris saw an increasing number of Belgian refugees, some arriving in cars with mattresses tied to their roofs, others dragging heavy suitcases from Gare du

Nord, still others on bicycles. Although the French professed faith in their army, that faith was dashed when the Germans broke through the Maginot Line. Air-raid alerts, coupled with near black-outs each night, fuelled rumours that soon the Germans would be in the Paris suburbs and, soon after that, in the city. By 16 May 1940 news of Germany's advances had incited a feeling of panic. Two days later, the French learned that Prime Minister Paul Reynaud had taken over the Ministry of National Defence, ousting his rival Édouard Daladier. Reynaud called upon the 84-year-old Marshal Pétain (a hero of the First World War, a paternal and popular figure), and the stubborn and outspoken General Maxime Weygand: both men – who had seen victory for France in 1918 – had been summoned to plan strategy. The hope of counter-attacks buoyed French spirits, but that hope lasted only for days: Holland had surrendered; Belgium had surrendered. In early June, 250 planes dropped leaflets on Paris, promising to bomb the city the next day. German bombers were met by French anti-aircraft fire, but Germany's losses were not severe enough to deter them. On 14 June, Nazi tanks invaded Paris. By then, air-raid alerts and the blackest rumours had emptied the city once again.

According to Madsen, Chanel left Paris in early June, driven by a chauffeur to Pau near the Pyrénées, where she had bought a house for the family of her nephew André Palasse – an early conscript who, she learned, had been taken as a prisoner of war. If she had planned to 'keep still' during a long stay, she changed her mind within weeks: France fell to the Germans, an armistice was signed on 21 June, and Paris was declared an open city. She decided to return, travelling this time in the company of the feisty Marie-Louise Bousquet, a woman she saw occasionally in the company of their many mutual friends. With stops in Vichy, Moulins and Bourbon-L'Archambault, sleeping wherever they could and procuring petrol whenever they were able, the two women arrived back in Paris at the end of August.

Chanel headed immediately to the Ritz. When she discovered that Germans were occupying her apartment, she demanded a room, and the Ritz became her own headquarters until the end of the war. Misia criticized her for consorting with the enemy, but many Parisians who lived at the Ritz resumed their lives there, and merely residing in the same hotel was not evidence of collaboration. Her boutique remained open so that the building would avoid being requisitioned by the Germans, but Chanel did not appear there. Other designers, however, saw the occupiers as an eager market. As Janet Flanner reported in the *New Yorker*, Germans were ravenous for French luxury goods:

Like termites that have been walled in for years and on a diet, the Germans, since the middle of June, have steadily advanced through the Paris shops, absorbing, munching, consuming lingerie, perfume, bonbons, leather goods, sweet silly novelties – all the chic, charm and *gourmandise* of Parisian merchandise.[16]

Officers' wives bought couture from those houses that remained open, even though the wartime fashions were made of ersatz materials such as rayon or acetate, rather than silk or wool. Although evening wear revived flounces and full skirts, outfits for the day reflected severe restrictions in yardage imposed by the Germans. Skirts were slim, with hems ending just below the knee. With leather restricted, shoes were made with wooden soles, or a mixture of bark and sisal; and leather handbags disappeared, substituted by oilcloth or fabric totes. Wool was in short supply during one of the coldest winters in memory, and French women scavenged among men's jackets and trousers to remake them into coats for themselves, or slit open down pillows for filling quilted jackets.

Hats became a coveted accessory: even those made by milliners were cheap, and many women began to make their own at home from any scraps they could salvage. Hats, in fact, became subversive political statements. Hats with bows, streamers and ribbons; hats embellished with spangles and embroidery; hats that towered precariously on the head: to French women they symbolized defiance and resistance against German strictures. 'Huge eccentric hats became the rage of Paris', wrote Hélène Lazareff. 'They were as eloquent as flags.'[17]

As the occupation went on, French designers felt threatened n two fronts: by German authorities who officially opposed Paris style on aesthetic and moral grounds, and wanted any designs sent first to Berlin for approval; and by rumours from America (where newspapers and magazines glorified the fashion industry flourishing in New York), which declared that Paris as the centre of fashion was finished. Throughout the summer and autumn of 1940 – with many fashionable women staying out of Paris and displays of elegance seeming in bad taste – designers pressed their clients once again to dress up. But the future of French fashion – particularly Chanel's future – seemed in peril. On 18 November 1940, the Museum of Costume Art in the Rockefeller Center opened an exhibition of 600 fashion drawings from the *New York Times*, a retrospective of Paris style during the period of 1932–40. 'It should be noted', pronounced an article in the *Times*, 'that the collection of sketches begins with the time when Paris was just delivering us from the long-waisted bodice and knee-length skirts of the post-war period – "a very ugly period"' according to museum official Polaire Weissman.[18] But that 'ugly period' was precisely Chanel's time of triumph – history, it seemed, was not being kind to her legacy.

8

Recluse

I cannot take orders from anyone else, except in love . . .
Chanel[1]

In Chanel's social circles, many treated the occupying Germans as
guests rather than enemies and welcomed officers into their homes.
Like some of those friends, Chanel was a stalwart conservative and
a proponent of order and discipline. The anti-Semitic views that
emerged during her relationship with Iribe could burst out at any
time, as she blamed Jews for everything – from France's political
troubles to bad weather; but those views, which may have been
superficial and thoughtless, did not preclude her friendships
with Hélène and Pierre Lazareff, or Maurice Sachs, or any of the
Rothschilds. Her affair with Hans Gunther von Dincklage, known
as Spatz ('the sparrow') seems less a reflection of her political
beliefs than her desire for love, companionship and protection.

She may have met Spatz long before the war. He had been in
Paris since 1928 working at the German embassy, and he had
earned a reputation as a playboy. Divorced in 1935, he had just
ended an affair when, according to several biographers, Chanel
sought him out, looking for information about her nephew André
Palasse who was a prisoner of war. Spatz identified himself as a
diplomat, but his role – both before and during the war– remains
mysterious: Charles-Roux claimed that Spatz was a spy, a member of
the Nazi counter-espionage agency. Horst thought he was a double

agent, working for both the Nazis and the British. Chanel was interested only in his attributes as a man: about twelve years younger than she, he was tall, blond and urbane. He was available, and so was she.

During the German occupation, she and Spatz spent most of their time in Paris with occasional trips to Roquebrune. Although theatres, cinemas and restaurants were open, the couple tried to live discreetly and quietly, preferring private dinners and parties. Her circle included Misia and José-Maria Sert who always kept their house open to friends, as well as Cocteau and his lover, the actor Jean Marais, the latter praising Chanel's generosity in sending cheering gifts to the soldiers in his company. Others with whom she socialized were openly supporters of the occupiers: Picasso, who sold paintings to wealthy Germans; Maurice Sachs, a Jew who became a secret member of the Gestapo; Paul Morand, on the Vichy payroll as president of the Film Censorship Board, and his wife, Hélène, who was pro-German and frequently entertained French sympathizers and German officers and their wives. Serge Lifar had been given the directorship of the Paris Opera ballet during the occupation, a position for which he felt considerable pride.

If Chanel's wartime behaviour seems consistent with that of many other Parisians, one episode stands out as especially odious: her opportunistic attempt to oust the Wertheimers from control of Les Parfums Chanel when the Commission of Jewish Affairs began to seize Jewish businesses and transfer their ownership to Aryans. After the Wertheimer brothers fled to America, Chanel saw her chance to reclaim her business by installing someone loyal to her as CEO. But the Wertheimers were one step ahead, placing Félix Amiot – a cousin and a non-Jewish aviation industri alist – as caretaker administrator. Amiot was able to produce a bill of sale to confirm his position. Moreover, years before, the brothers had set up a new company in New York, Chanel, Inc., which kept up both the manufacturing and advertising of perfumes and cosmetics throughout the war. Chanel's latest effort to undermine the Wertheimers once again was foiled.

Although the effort at least gave her something to occupy her mind, once she lost the case, she was left idle and restless. 'Nothing relaxes me so much as work', she told Paul Morand, 'and nothing tires me so much as doing nothing'.[2] She hardly worked during the German occupation but she saw others in fashion work hard, desperately putting out showings with rationed material and artificial fabrics. Those who found it difficult to keep up their fashion houses turned to designing for films and the theatre; many of Chanel's seamstresses, suddenly unemployed, managed to find jobs with costume designers. Chanel, isolated from the world of fashion, seemed very bored to her friends. Perhaps it was boredom that led her to believe she could end the war.

In the summer of 1943, when Germany began to suffer defeats in Russia and Africa, Chanel devised a plan: she would act as an envoy to Winston Churchill. He would listen to her, she convinced German Major Walter Schellenberg, on account of their old friendship, and she would persuade him to negotiate peace with Germany. The caper that came to be known as 'Operation Modellhut' involved Chanel travelling to Madrid where she would meet with Churchill, due to arrive there from the Middle East. Refusing to travel alone, she entreated Schellenberg to procure Vera Bate, whose Italian husband, Alberto Lombardi, was in hiding in Rome. A message delivered by a German officer to Bate in her Rome apartment informed her that Chanel needed her in Paris, where she was about to reopen her business. Bate, astonished, refused the invitation; with her husband preparing to join the Allies in Italy, she was not about to leave the country with a German. But a few weeks later, Bate was arrested by the Gestapo in Rome, accused of spying for the British. Within weeks, Schellenberg arranged for Bate's release, and again she was informed that Chanel needed her in Paris. This time, she agreed to go.

While it is not clear whether Bate believed that Chanel was reopening her business or knew the diplomatic plan, she nevertheless thought that once in Madrid she could seek help from the British embassy in arranging safe transport to her family in England. Chanel was satisfied to have a travelling companion, and in November she and Bate checked into the Ritz in Madrid and separately proceeded to interviews at the British embassy. What happened there remains, like much of this escapade, blurred. Chanel disclosed her plan to speak to Churchill as soon as he arrived in Madrid. Bate, for her part, apparently insisted to the officer who interviewed her that Chanel was a German agent who had duped her into accompanying her to Madrid on the pretext of opening her fashion house there. Bate may have been aware of Chanel's relationship with Spatz; she may have wanted to distance herself from any plan to negotiate with the Germans. For whatever reason, Bate decided to betray the woman who once was a close and trusted friend.

Churchill never arrived in Madrid: he had become ill in Cairo and was taken to Eisenhower's headquarters in Tunisia to recover. Chanel had no choice but to head back to Paris; Bate, however, refused to leave, hoping still to gain passage to England. In Paris, when Chanel learned of Bate's betrayal, she confessed that she was wounded and incredulous: in her own eyes, she had done nothing wrong. 'I could not become rabid on the Italian subject, or, on the German subject, hear or say low things which I leave to the retarded. To scorn your enemy is to debase yourself', she wrote to Bate in December. Nor, she said, had she left Spain under anyone's orders: 'I have given a lot of them in my life and not taken any yet. But my visa was up. S. [apparently Schellenberg] was afraid I might have problems.'[3]

Chanel's next step involved meeting Schellenberg in Berlin, which occurred early in 1944. Why she went, what their conversation entailed – all that has been lost to history. Not long after the two met, the Allies landed in Normandy and by summer the Germans were fleeing from Paris. Spatz left for Switzerland; Chanel, still believing herself immune to reprobation, stayed at the Ritz. If she thought that her affair with Spatz and her failed 'Operation Modellhut' had no consequences, she soon found out differently. One September morning in 1944, Chanel was arrested on the orders of the Committee of Public Morals. She was questioned for three hours, during which she was asked about Spatz, whom she admitted having known for twenty years. She said he told her that he was going to Germany. Did she confess that they were lovers? Did she talk about her peace plan? Although she said little about the interrogation afterwards, she always maintained that her behaviour in closing down her fashion house was more patriotic than those designers who kept working during the occupation. Perhaps she made that case to her interlocutors.

Because of Chanel's quick release, biographers have speculated that she had information that could have embarrassed Winston Churchill, who was due in Paris for ceremonies to commemorate the armistice. Madsen speculates that Churchill had arranged with the Germans to protect an apartment in Paris owned by the Duke of Windsor. With Chanel's testimony, in fact, the Windsors themselves might have been exposed as collaborators. Charles-Roux suggests that a high-placed official had orders to protect her. Chanel decided to believe that her arrest was a result of her offending the Syndicat de la Couture by closing her business during the war.

While other women who consorted with Germans were paraded naked through the streets, and some faced imprisonment, Chanel was free. She left for Switzerland almost immediately, and except for occasional visits to France and a few trips to America she lived mostly in Lausanne for the next eight years, sometimes in the company of Spatz. Her ease in getting a visa to travel abroad seems further evidence that someone influential was protecting her. In

Lausanne, Chanel stayed at the Beau Rivage Hotel on Lac Leman, frequented by aged exiles from South America and central Europe. In the hotel reception room, one visitor remembered, Romanian, Greek and Argentinean women played cards in a cloud of cigarette smoke; the clientele was content to live cut off from the world under the watch of vigilant staff, tremulously holding in pale, wrinkled hands their copies of the *Financial Times* or the *Wall Street Journal*. Among this decrepit community, Chanel stood out as healthy and energetic.[4] Even after she bought a small house in Lausanne, she often spent her days at the hotel.

Although she claimed to like the Swiss because they worked hard and stayed out of wars, it was also true that her Swiss doctors supplied her with the narcotics she depended on (sleeping pills and painkillers); besides, she had her sizeable bank account in Switzerland. Jean Cocteau wrote in his diary,

> Saw Chanel, who tells me about her Swiss residency: she no longer pays taxes in France, only a Swiss fine. But for those of us who are not so rich as she, the advantage would be offset by the cost of life in Switzerland. The money would disappear just as fast as it does in taxes.[5]

But her money had grown during the war, thanks to royalties deposited by the Wertheimers from their thriving perfume business. They had bought a factory in New Jersey and continued to manu-facture and promote Chanel No. 5, as well as additional scents: Chanel No. 22, named for the year it was created; Gardénia, 1925; Bois des Îles, 1926, and Cuir de Russie, the company's most masculine scent, created in 1928. Other scents – Le Beige de Chanel, Le Bleu de Chanel and Le Rouge de Chanel, Ivoire de Chanel and Glamour – had been promoted briefly in the 1930s and early '40s but disappeared before the war. Chanel No. 5 was by far the most popular with women who bought it for themselves,

GI soldiers outside Chanel's boutique following the liberation of Paris, 1945.

and especially with men buying gifts. Amid a proliferation of sometimes unpronounceable names, Chanel No. 5 still stood out. And the scent – dominated as it was by aldehyde – seemed even more current in the 1940s than it had been twenty years before.[6]

Chanel, however, was not mollified by a royalty cheque for £10,000, which she suspected was far too low, nor about news of a revised recipe for her coveted perfume. She saw yet another opportunity to attack the Wertheimers and decided to manufacture her own perfumes, give them slightly different names and compete with the brothers. In addition, she sued them for bringing out an inferior product and demanded that all rights revert to her. René de Chambrun – whose father-in-law Pierre Laval had been executed as a collaborator – hoped to keep a low profile after his return to Paris from America, where he spent the war. Still, he agreed to represent his famous client's interests in negotiations with a frustrated Pierre Wertheimer. If Chanel could not have power in her business, she wanted money. In the end, she emerged with 2 per cent of worldwide perfume and cosmetic sales, which guaranteed her £37,000 and more every year. With her share of worldwide sales, the company increased its £10,000 cheque in royalties from the war years to the amount of £200,000 – worth several millions of pounds today.

Occasionally, she and Spatz went to Paris to attend the opera or visit a diminishing number of friends. Her world was becoming smaller and smaller: she suspected that some ostracized her because of her relationship with Spatz. Also, several of her contemporaries had died: Max Jacob succumbed during the war; Dmitri, whose friendship endured long after their love affair ended, died shortly after the occupation; José-Maria Sert died in 1947. Paul Morand was in self-imposed exile in Switzerland, a victim of his opportunistic collaboration with the Gestapo. Misia was nearly blind and very frail. Along with the loss of her friends came her perceived loss of fame. 'People like us don't need advice; we need approval', she told Dalí. 'Celebrity is loneliness, isn't it?'[7] Hungry for approval and recognition, she sought ways to remind the world that she still existed. A book, she thought, might do that: for that project, she needed a writer.

Her first try was with Louise de Vilmorin, an aristocratic and caustic *femme de lettres*, who met Chanel in 1947. Chanel's idea was to produce a memoir that could serve as the basis for a film adaptation of her life. Recurring themes, Vilmorin noted immediately, were her obsession with money as the essential means to freedom, women's will and independence from men, and women's sly talent to manipulate while pretending to be manipulated.[8] She created a story of her childhood to reflect back on her own image: she said her father wanted a larger world than the Auvergne, and she idealized her parents as having inherent good taste for what was clean, fresh and luxurious.[9] Vilmorin found it impossible to divert Chanel from the indelible, scripted version of her life, and she soon lost interest in the project.

After Chanel's death, Vilmorin published *Mémoires de Coco*, portraying her would-be subject as self-serving and narcissistic.

In the early 1950s, Chanel agreed to work with Cocteau's friend André Fraigneau,[10] but when that didn't work out she then collaborated with Michel Déon. Both of these projects failed because of Chanel's insistence on repeating the fictions she had created, stories that could not help but sound like part of a publicity campaign. Despite an inability to work together, Chanel and Déon became friends, and she often invited him to dine with her. One day, Déon was walking along Lac Leman when he met Henri Mondor, a renowned surgeon and historian of French literature, whose works included studies of Mallarmé and Valéry. Upon hearing about the encounter, Chanel asked Déon to invite Mondor – whom she had met briefly before the war – to lunch. What Déon did not anticipate was Chanel's enormous antipathy to Mondor once she remembered that he was from the Auvergne. When he began to reminisce about the region, she tried to change the conversation immediately, and then began to attack brutally the poets he so championed. Mondor was abashed and visibly upset. Déon believed that Chanel's cruelty stemmed from her fear that Mondor's reminiscences of the Auvergne would contradict her mythological version of her youth.

Chanel was in Lausanne in the autumn of 1950 when she learned that Misia's health was rapidly failing. Rushing to Paris, she barely arrived on time to see her most intimate friend die. In a rare gesture of tenderness, she asked to be left alone with the body and proceeded to dress Misia in white, festoon her with jewels, comb her hair and apply make-up: Chanel readied the elegant Misia for her mourners. Despite arguments, misunderstandings and rivalry, Chanel had loved Misia and her death meant the loss of the person who understood her most profoundly. Other deaths were to soon follow in the next few years: Spatz, Étienne Balsan and Bendor.

One friendship that endured was that with Cocteau, perhaps because he refused to take offence at her cattiness. After lunching with her at Roquebrune in 1951, Cocteau described her in his diaries: 'She protests inveterately and against everything. Her little black swan's head. One of those Auvergnats with Romany grandparents. Her gypsy style . . . that look of an Auvergnat gypsy.'[11]Although Chanel denigrated him publicly because he had attained more fame than her beloved Reverdy, she continued to dine with him, nurture him and help him – sometimes with astounding generosity. 'I don't lend money, I give it', she said. 'It costs the same.'[12] Often she stubbornly refused, even if long-time friends asked. When Serge Lifar needed money to buy the curtains from *Parade* that Picasso had designed, Chanel would neither give nor lend.[13] But rarely did she refuse Cocteau. When boxer Panama Al Brown, Cocteau's lover, needed drug treatment so he could return to the ring, she paid. When Brown came out, he asked her for help again and she found him a trainer, agreeing to pay as long as he trained seriously. 'You're a fallen champion', she told him. 'No one wants to see you any more. Win again, and you'll have everyone at your feet.' This advice could have been what she said to herself as she struggled to revive her reputation. When Brown returned to the ring, she watched a match; in the third round, he winked at her and delivered a knock-out.

Friends who saw her in the 1950s, as she neared 70, noted that she seemed vastly different from the woman they knew before the war. Horst visited her in New York in December 1951, when she travelled there with Maggie van Zuylen, with whom she stayed at the Waldorf Astoria. 'I think Chanel was somewhat lost at that time of her life', Horst recalled: 'she seemed bored. Her hair was different and she had started to pluck her eyebrows. She didn't look like the Chanel I had known.' She spent a day at Horst's house in Oyster Bay. He photographed her in his Manhattan studio but the results were disappointing for both of them. Although they agreed to do another sitting some other time, that time never came, and she refused to be photographed again, preferring her glamorous 1937 portraits.[14]

He met up with Chanel again in Rome the following year, where she seemed more relaxed. Recognized whenever she went out, she coveted attention. One night, at dinner, she wore a slinky black cocktail dress under a full-length fur coat, with a black ribbon tied in her hair. Just as when she was younger, the elegant, simple gown stood out among women more opulently and colourfully dressed. 'As she entered the restaurant, heads turned', Horst recalled, and conversations stopped as diners gaped at her jewellery of gold and fake gems.

He visited her every time he was in Paris, and she seemed glad to see him. They usually had a simple lunch, with a bottle of chilled white wine, set on a table with batiste napkins. Chanel held forth in a monologue, devastatingly catty and critical. She seemed consumed by loneliness, Horst decided, repeating the same two-hour rendition of her wartime experiences (without mention of Spatz) whenever they met for dinner at the Ritz. These encounters made Horst sad – but also irritated, as he stood with his hand on the door handle, longing to escape.

If Chanel had thoughts of returning to business, she must have realized how challenging that would be just after the war: materials for dressmaking – even pins and needles – were in short supply. Wool was scarce, fur was non-existent and a dress could use no more than 2–3 m (6½–10 ft) of fabric. It was difficult to find workers and mannequins were terribly thin from malnourishment. Also, the value of the franc was falling, making clothing strikingly expensive.

Schiaparelli, who had by that time returned from America, responded to stringency by slimming down her styles, designing a line with dropped shoulders and high bosoms. 'In short', she said, 'we reversed the Occupation line'. She also made what she called 'flat dresses with sloping lines, easily packed, easily carried, light in weight and becoming to the figure', in the style of Chinese clothing.[15] Within a few years, though, with fabrics more readily available, Paris revived. Designers discovered that women wanted luxury once more, and buyers finally returned to the showrooms. One impediment to the fashion industry's quick recovery was a new law imposed in 1947 by the Syndicat de la Couture that put restrictions on copying. Before the war, buyers could go to whatever shows they pleased, buy whatever they wanted and have models copied freely. Their advertisements promoted the names of famous designers, giving them free publicity. But with the new laws, this freedom was curtailed. Because an entrance fee was required for each show, buyers visited fewer of them. With photographers banned from shows, designers found that their audiences shrank. With devalued currency, clothing costs rose shockingly high. 'The twenty-five franc dress', Schiaparelli recalled, 'which startled me in 1945, quickly became a 100,000 franc dress, a 200,000 franc or 300,000 franc dress' – £185 to £560. With American import duties, the price became prohibitive.[16]

French designers noted that in New York the easy availability of fabric inspired extravagance: jackets were enhanced by peplums, sleeves ballooned into leg-of-mutton shapes that had not been seen since the 1890s and full skirts cascaded from tiny waists. Designers noticed, too, that fashion was changing not only in style: the war had injected a new democratization into women's clothing. Street wear of slim suits and frivolous hats was available to all women, regardless of class. Even women who could afford couture clothing increasingly bought ready-to-wear. Movies, rising in popularity as mass entertainment, powerfully influenced women who had once taken their fashion cues from socialites. Now, they coveted wardrobes worn by the likes of Claudette Colbert, Hedy Lamarr, Greer Garson and Bette Davis; Hollywood costume designers took a new role as arbiters of fashion.

Paris, though, was hardly finished as the centre of elegance, as Chanel discovered in February 1947 when Christian Dior presented his first collection. Although the 42-year-old designer paid homage to her, Molyneux and Lucien Lelong, his collection, which he called *Corolle* (flower petal), seemed as fresh as Chanel's little black sheath had been in 1926. Dresses featured cinched waists, voluminous skirts, hemlines lowered to 30 cm (12 in.) from the floor. Fabric was available again, and Dior revelled in metres and metres of it. Carmel Snow, entranced, called the style the 'New Look', two words that became more than an epithet: they were a kind of blessing. Department stores bought dozens of outfits, sometimes 40 each, as well as Dior's accessories: gloves, handbags, jewellery and hats. For the New Look, Dior had in mind a new woman, with a full bust, hand-span waists and round hips; a woman eager to flaunt a new definition of femininity; most of all, a woman who yearned to forget the stringencies and hardships of war.

9

Roped by Pearls

Ageing is Adam's charm and Eve's tragedy.
Chanel[1]

Rage and boredom: those were the reasons that Chanel gave for
returning to *couture*. Both may have been true. Her rage, while
focused on Dior's 'New Look', could have been fuelled just as
well by 40-year-old Pierre Balmain, whose fashion house opened
in 1945; or 32-year-old Pierre Cardin, or 27-year-old Hubert de
Givenchy, both of whom had just launched their own labels in
1953. It could even have been fuelled by 60-year-old Cristóbal
Balenciaga, whom Chanel admired and whose house had remained
open throughout the war. Like Dior, Balenciaga's post-war collection
of exquisitely sleek, elegant designs inspired accolades. She was
angry too, she said repeatedly, because women were being dressed
by men who detested women: in other words, by gay designers,
such as Dior.

Her view was clearly in the minority but Chanel, Bettina Ballard
observed,

> lived a very protected fashion life . . . surrounded by a court of
> friends who thought the way she thought, dressed the way she
> dressed, and disapproved of any other conception of fashion as
> she did.[2]

Dior, after all, had become the media's darling. In the years between his opening in 1947 and hers in 1954, his style rapidly evolved and his reputation soared. His clientele eagerly awaited the ever-changing, ever-new looks. 'A collection is created in two months, and the fashion dies and must die quickly', he said. Unlike Chanel, whose style was identifiable from season to season, Dior featured an innovative line for every collection: Vertical, Trompe L'Oeil, Mid-Century, Sinuous, Oblique, Oval, Princesse, Tulip, Cupola . . . Photographed for *Vogue* by Horst and Irving Penn, Dior's clothing looked sumptuously, sensuously chic. Dior, *Vogue* wrote, offered 'beautifully designed, desirable clothes with the fixed purpose of interesting, of dramatizing a woman'.[3] Chanel feared that with every burst of applause for Dior, she was being forgotten by her once adoring public.

In 1949, a Gallup Poll rated Dior the fifth best-known man in the world; fashion commentators announced that he had begun a revolution. Modest as he was, he conceded that the New Look reflected a new mood 'that sought refuge from the mechanical and impersonal in a return to tradition . . . The woman of 1925, her hat jammed down to her eyebrows, looked like the machine from which the music and decoration of the period took their inspiration. Nowadays we are afraid of the female robot.' His styles, he added, were an effort to 'defend every inch of our own personal luxury'.[4] But Chanel saw him as anachronistic, forcing women into a role that she and others had renounced: the woman as decorative object, adorned in uncomfortable clothing so stiff that dresses could stand by themselves. Of course, women want to look attractive, she conceded, but 'designers have forgotten that there are women inside the dresses', women who want 'to move, to get into a car without bursting their seams!'[5]

Other than yearning to reclaim her position in fashion, Chanel had deeply emotional reasons to return to designing. For her, work was an anodyne more powerful than any of her pills: 'I don't know what I'm trying to forget', she told Dalí, 'maybe that I'm alive. And I keep moving to pretend that I'm trying to catch up with time.'[6] She surely felt isolated and ignored; and she was afraid that without work, she would lose her prized slenderness: 'If a woman wants to keep her figure, let her be employed, let her work', she told writer Djuna Barnes years before. 'She will be happier, less self-conscious, and this state will be reflected in the figure.'[7] Without work she felt lost. 'If I didn't work, what would you like me to do?' she asked journalist Jacques Chazot during an interview. 'Play cards all day like three-quarters of women? I'm not crazy!'[8]

Besides rage, boredom and jealousy, she may have had a financial incentive to reopen her fashion house: among the stories that have been put forth about her comeback, one has it that Pierre Wertheimer visited Chanel in 1953 and told her that sales of No. 5 were falling. He encouraged her to resume designing – and in fact offered her financial backing – in order to revive attention to the brand. Pierre Galante told a variation of that story: Chanel asked for backing but when Wertheimer showed no interest, she manipulated him into supporting her by threatening to design for an American wholesaler – just as Dior had done in 1948 when he opened a ready-to-wear store in New York. Even with the sale of La Pausa in 1953, Chanel did not have enough money for a comeback; with an American backer, though, she could sidestep the Wertheimers completely. Not surprisingly, according to Galante, Wertheimer took her threat seriously and agreed to finance her.[9] Axel Madsen asserts that the deal gave Wertheimer 100 per cent of Chanel Couture, including all real estate holdings and textile production: in exchange for backing her return, he bought her out completely.

During the years leading up to her comeback, Chanel focused on Dior as the kind of rival Patou had been in the 1920s and Schiaparelli in the 1930s. Although Dior had grown up as the privileged son of a wealthy chemical fertilizer manufacturer, attended a fashionable Paris prep school before opening his own art gallery and learned designing by working for Lucien Lelong and Robert Piguet, he – like Chanel – set up his business with the help of a wealthy man: cotton magnate Marcel Boussac. Like Chanel, his success came quickly and he enhanced his renown by diversifying first into fragrances (establishing Christian Dior Perfumes in 1949) and soon into ready-to-wear clothing (setting up eight companies in all, including those that manufactured hosiery and shoes). By the autumn of 1954, his conglomerate was grossing an annual income of £10.5 million. Beginning with three workrooms and 85 employees in 1946, he expanded to five buildings, 25 workrooms and 1,200 employees, some of whom worked in his manufacturing plant in Venezuela. As superstitious as Chanel – he consulted fortune-tellers and believed 8 was his lucky number – 'Papa Dior' (as his staff affectionately called him) proved to be the right man at the right time. Chanel hoped that the time was right for her, too.

Could Chanel make a successful comeback? 'Last week all fashion-conscious Paris was asking this question as it trooped once again to Rue Cambon for 71-year-old Coco Chanel's first fashion show in 15 years', *Time* reported. 'There was more than a show of feline claws as the fat cats of the fashion world crowded in among the models like subway riders in rush hour.' According to Bettina Ballard, although Chanel felt ill as she finished her collection of 130 models, she let nothing stop her.[10] She was determined to present her showing on 5 February, invoking her lucky number.

At the showing, Chanel perched at the top of the stairs as usual, sure that the press was hostile to her. She watched tensely as her models paraded through the crowded salon, each holding the number of the outfit – except for no. 13. Unlike other designers, Chanel did not ascribe flowery names to her styles, a practice she thought pretentious. Her audience, in any case, needed no names; what they saw were Chanel's iconic styles: the cardigan suit, the

Marie-Hélène Arnaud in a Chanel suit, 1959.

boater hat, the lace cocktail dresses that had seemed so charming in the 1920s and '30s. Her models were as slender and small-boned as in the past, and the most alluring among them was nineteen-year-old Marie-Hélène Arnaud – Chanel's favourite, and, some came to believe, apparent heir to the fashion house.

Although a few friends rushed to congratulate her afterwards, Chanel sensed disappointment and she sequestered herself for the rest of the evening. By the next day, her feelings were confirmed: the consensus, at least in Paris, was dismay. The designs seemed dowdy as did some of the models. Dior's models swished and swayed; Chanel's seemed demure in comparison. 'It was touching; one might have thought oneself back in 1925', *Le Figaro* remarked.[11] Fashion observers expected a revolution; after all, that was her reputation in the 1920s. But Chanel was not the bright young thing she had been then; and, as she admitted, she designed for herself. She was convinced, though, that her contemporaries would rally around her. 'The women will understand me', she said, more hopeful than confident.[12]

Although most of the French press hated the showing, Chanel was saved by the Americans. Bettina Ballard, who was covering the Paris openings for American *Vogue*, praised the collection in a spread that featured Arnaud in a navy jersey suit – much like Ballard's favourite Chanel suit before the war. Lord & Taylor and B. Altman bought some outfits; Hattie Carnegie bought some too. Carmel Snow effusively praised Chanel's comeback, commissioning a piece by Cocteau to run in *Harper's Bazaar*'s March issue, along with a portrait of Chanel by photographer Louise Dahl-Wolfe.

Between her first showing in February and her second on 5 October 1954, fashion commentators came around to Snow's opinion: Chanel was as astute as always, intuiting the needs of a new generation of women. In March, an international fashion show at the Waldorf-Astoria revealed Chanel's influence already permeating the work of other designers. A casual look predominated, reported Ballard, evident in Dior's jackets, Givenchy's shirtwaist dresses and Balenciaga's loose waistlines. In the summer, Dior innovated once again, this time drawing unexpected criticism from the press. 'World of Fashion Is Divided on Dior', the *New York Times* announced. The designer who seemed to adore women's curves

suddenly preferred a new 'flat look' that required an undergarment
that compressed the breasts, much like what women wore in the
1920s. In fact, nothing that Dior designed – from the beginning
of his career – could be worn without appropriate shaping undergarments, but his newest direction shocked many of his fans. 'My
dream', he once said, 'is to save women from nature'.[13] This was
precisely Chanel's objection.

The styles with which Chanel is most strongly identified
(excluding the famous little black dress) all come from her revival
in the 1950s: the two-toned sling-back shoe designed by Chanel
with the exclusive House of Massaro (shoemakers to Elizabeth
Taylor and the Duchess of Windsor); the quilted bag[14] in Chanel's
signature colours of black, red for the lining and a shade of beige
that, she said, evoked the wet sands at Deauville when the tide
was going out; and the slim-skirted suit with a boxy, hip-length,
collarless jacket. These three pieces of clothing became synonymous with Chanel and they became coveted, just as she predicted.

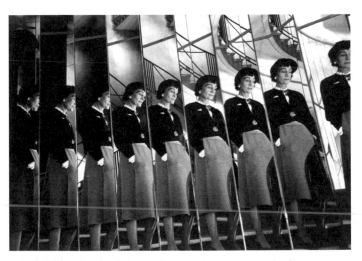

Chanel standing in front of the mirrored staircase in her salon, photographed by
Robert Doisneau, 1954.

Chanel fitting a model in 1954.

Actresses such as Jeanne Moreau, Delphine Seyrig, Elizabeth Taylor and Grace Kelly photographed in Chanel outfits gave them a new aura of glamour. With her revival, film directors – including Louis Malle, Roger Vadim and Alain Resnais – asked her to design costumes for their productions. Richard Avedon and Irving Penn photographed her designs for *Vogue* and *Harper's Bazaar*.

Her return to business energized Chanel as she entered her eighth decade. Although she often protested that awards meant nothing to her, in September 1957 she travelled to Dallas, Texas, to receive the Neiman-Marcus Golden Anniversary Plaque, a fashion world honour. Reporting on the event, the *New York Times* described her as a 'bird-like French woman of 74 years, with eyes like two black sequins and the air of an impish schoolgirl'. Her special style, the paper said, 'is compounded from three ingredients: girlishness, comfort, and a generous helping of pearls. In a country where the emphasis is on youth and free and easy living, her designs were bound to succeed.' After her 1954 opening, her influence once again 'spread quickly, partly because Chanel, unlike other members of the French couture, likes to be copied'. The article was accompanied by drawings of 'authentic copies' available at Bonwit Teller, Lord & Taylor and Bergdorf Goodman. The prices were nowhere near *haute couture*: a wool suit at Lord & Taylor sold for £23.50; a satin theatre suit cost £62 at Bergdorf Goodman.[15] Couture models cost ten times those prices.

Although the *New York Times* celebrated Chanel as a personality, an article just a few months before made it clear that for a new generation of women Chanel was an adjective describing a style. 'The Chanel look', the *Times* said

named for a French designer of the Nineteen Twenties, varies slightly from showroom to showroom but generally features looser lines and semi-fitted box jackets, particularly in crepe and jersey fabrics. The Chanel influence is reported throughout the dress market, even in children's sizes.[16]

Stopping in Manhattan, she was interviewed for a piece in the *New Yorker*, where she admitted that 'the grand problem' in designing 'is to rejuvenate women. To make women look young. Then their outlook on life changes. They feel more joyous.'[17] Youthfulness had been her mantra in the 1930s; it was her mantra still.

While she was in the United States, Chanel heard some shocking news: her rival Dior had died from a massive heart attack while vacationing in Montecatini, Italy. Although the overweight designer had suffered heart attacks in the past, his death at 52 still stunned the fashion world. The future of his company, though, was never in doubt: within weeks, Dior's protégé, 21-year-old Yves Saint-Laurent,

Chanel, wool and silk suit, *c.* 1958.

was named as his successor. 'Saint-Laurent has excellent taste', Chanel remarked after his first collection appeared. 'The more he copies me, the better taste he displays.'[18] Now Chanel had a new rival.

In 1959, *Saks News* – the house newsletter of Saks Fifth Avenue – reported that the merchandise manager for the exclusive Fifth Floor collections visited Paris from 22 January to 5 February, when designers had their openings. Dior, Lanvin, Pierre Cardin, Balenciaga, Patou, Givenchy, Jacques Fath and Chanel were among the houses that competed for his purchases. Among them, Chanel was a survivor. Dior had been replaced by Saint-Laurent, Patou had died in 1936, Lanvin in 1946, Fath in 1954; new designers had taken over these houses. But Chanel seemed indefatigable and as eager as ever before to see her styles copied and popularized.

From 1955 to 1971 she produced 30 collections, each showing about 80 models. When she was working on a collection, she would arrive at rue Cambon between ten and eleven in the morning, dressed in a suit, silk blouse and always her hat. By the 1960s, she had difficulty cutting because of arthritis (although even at the age of 65 she was still able to touch her hands to the floor without bending her knees) and she could work for about nine hours without resting, eating, drinking or, witnesses claim, going to the toilet. At eight o'clock, or sometimes later, she finally stopped for the day.

Her hard work, however, could not overcome the reality that the fashion business had entered a new age of ready-to-wear. Chanel, Inc. relied on cosmetic sales, especially perfume, for its profits. In 1956, Jacques Helleu joined the company as director of advertising for perfumes and cosmetics. Brilliant and astute, he created a series of stunningly successful campaigns in which glamorous women served as the 'face' of Chanel. Helleu understood the advertising allure of the cover girl – soon to be called a supermodel – and during his long tenure at the company, his choices included

Catherine Deneuve, Nicole Kidman, Vanessa Paradis, Keira Knightley and Kate Moss. Among the most memorable was Suzy Parker.

Parker – the tall, red-headed Texas native – did not fit the mould of Chanel's usual petite mannequins but she radiated energy and elegance, and she had a dazzling, irresistible smile. Photographed by Horst and Richard Avedon, Parker began her modelling career in 1948 at the age of fifteen, working with the Eileen Ford Agency, which represented her older sister Dorian. For the next ten years, she appeared regularly in *Vogue* and *Harper's Bazaar*, and was a star in Chanel's *cabine* until her marriage in 1958. Parker was not only a model though; she also embarked on a film career, appearing opposite such leading men as Cary Grant and Gary Cooper. Her impetuous and spirited personality was the inspiration for Audrey Hepburn's character in *Funny Face*. In 1957, Parker and Chanel appeared on the cover of *Elle*, coinciding with Chanel's Neiman-Marcus award ceremony. One of Chanel's personal favourites, Parker inspired rumours of Chanel's sexual attraction to her, rumours hotly denied by both. Their friendship was exceptionally warm and in 1959 Chanel became godmother to Parker's daughter, Georgia Belle Florian Coco Chanel de la Salle.

Beginning in the 1960s, Lilou Grumbach Marquand played an increasingly significant role in Chanel's life, and her memoir *Chanel M'a Dit* serves as a source for understanding Chanel's last years. Marquand – then married to newspaperman Philippe Grumbach – met Chanel through their mutual friends Hervé Mille, director of *Paris-Match*, and his brother, decorator Gérard Mille. After ordering an outfit from Chanel, Marquand suggested that instead of paying for it in cash, she reimburse her by working. Chanel agreed and Marquand took up a position first as press secretary, and later as companion, until Chanel's death. She said that for the first two years she saw little of Chanel because Marie-Hélène Arnaud, Chanel's cherished model, served as an intermediary between Chanel and anyone who threatened to get close to her. Although Chanel went to great lengths to keep Arnaud – even installing her father as head of the corporation – Arnaud finally left, with the ambition of starting her own fashion house. That project, and her attempts at an acting career, never fulfilled her dreams.

Chanel's relationship with Marquand can best be described as mercurial. At first, she seemed interested in everything about Marquand and her life, happy to find out what they shared, but Marquand was not sure her interest was sincere. 'Mademoiselle wanted to seduce me', Marquand remembered; 'no one could resist her'. At times, Chanel could be funny, attentive, passionate; but she could also be demanding, controlling and possessive. Marquand quickly learned that Chanel had opinions about everything: 'fashion, but also the way to breathe, to run, to nourish oneself'.[19]

Marquand's role quickly grew from business assistant to personal attendant. Every day, she arrived at the Ritz to do Chanel's hair and help her with her make-up. Jeanne, her maid, would then help her dress, and Chanel would apply perfume at several stages of the dressing process. They would leave the Ritz around 12.30 p.m., talking about the day's schedule. A flurry of activity preceded their entrance into the fashion house as the staff took their requisite places in the salon and atelier. At one o'clock, the workers would go to lunch at the canteen but Chanel was rarely hungry so early. She would sometimes make a surprise visit to the mannequins' *cabine*, or to the changing rooms if there were famous clients. Some clients – Brigitte Bardot, for example – preferred to avoid her.

Marquand dined at the Ritz with Chanel about twice a week. Chanel drank Sancerre, Marquand champagne. At the corner of the table, there was a small dish of cloves, and after every meal Chanel would put one under her tongue. 'She was extremely sensitive to odours', Marquand said, 'and could not stand the idea of bad breath'.[20] As she got older, her aversion to food odours increased, and at the Ritz she needed to sit several tables apart from other diners.

Part of Marquand's interest in the position was glamour: at dinners, she might meet fashion editor Diana Vreeland; writer Michel Déon; Jean-Jacques Servan-Schreiber, who came with Françoise Giroud, one of Chanel's clients; famous actors and actresses, such as Marlon Brando and Jeanne Moreau. Marquand recalled that Chanel seemed especially at ease with Marlene Dietrich, who shared recipes and make-up advice with her.

Like everyone else who spent time with Chanel during these years, Marquand remembered the incessant talking. 'At work, at table, in bed, out walking or in the car, in the Rue Cambon or elsewhere, Mademoiselle talked . . . She talked without stopping, without inhaling, prolonging lunches until five o'clock and dinners until dawn.' She was afraid of silence. When she talked, she couldn't keep her hands still, folding her napkin, fiddling with her knife at the table or, in her living room, a jade frog. In bed, she stroked her sheet or blanket. As she talked, she seemed to take inventory of her possessions, even the pearls in her necklace.[21]

By the 1960s, Marquand noticed, Chanel was revising her own history – even the lies that she had perpetuated so faithfully throughout her life.

> She said she didn't really love Boy Capel, who had shaped and launched her . . . She swore that the Grand-Duke Dmitri, her lover before the war, had dissuaded her from adopting a baby; that she had provoked the death of Paul Iribe . . . by making him join a tennis party after an illness; that finally she would have married the Duke of Westminster if she had been able to have a baby.[22]

She told Marquand that she had an affair with Dalí before the war, solely to annoy Gala. These contradictory and improbable confessions, Marquand thought, proved one thing: solitude weighed heavily on her.

When Marquand accompanied her to Italy or Switzerland for a vacation, her butler François Mironnet drove the Cadillac while Chanel – seated in the back with Marquand – would sing pieces from opera or songs of Yvonne Printemps, remembered from before the First World War. Chanel seemed happy on these excursions, but once inside her house in Lausanne she became restless and bored. Often, she and Marquand read side by side, or Chanel would ask her to read a poem or take a walk with her, but she would then plunge into depression. She hated vacations.

What she loved, other than work, was meddling in other people's lives. 'To the question, "What would you have been in another life?" Chanel would always answer, "surgeon." Because she was curious about illnesses', Marquand said, 'but also, I believe, for her liking to interfere'. Claude Delay, for example, remembered Chanel's admonition to a young woman asking her advice about marriage:

When you marry a man you should think of it as if it was your first child. He's very fragile! When he comes home harassed and doesn't like the sample of skyblue wallpaper you show him for your bedroom, don't try to be in the right. You should never say no to him.[23]

Marquand remembered when Romy Schneider came to see Chanel (sent by Visconti). Chanel took her into the salon, watched her move and made her diagnosis. She told Romy to diet, cut her hair; she loved the role of Pygmalion.[24]

She was forthright about interfering in Marquand's life, too. When her husband wanted to leave Paris in 1962 and move to Provence, Chanel disapproved. At the time, the move seemed to give Marquand a chance to escape what by then was Chanel's exploitation of her: demanding so much time and commitment that Marquand was forced to neglect her family; sometimes erupting into a rage and firing her, then cajoling her to return. Nevertheless, when the

Romy Schneider
wearing Chanel
1962.

Marquands soon returned to Paris because they needed more
income, Marquand asked for her job back and Chanel rehired her.
Immediately, Marquand noted a change in Chanel's life: she seemed
to have fallen in love with François Mironnet, flirting with him
as if she were a young woman and talking of marrying him.
He resembled the Duke, she told Marquand, he made her feel
peaceful, and soon she promoted him to jewellery designer.
François, for his part, admired her but not as a romantic partner;
besides, he was engaged. When his fiancée came to Paris from
England, Chanel hired her as a maid to ensure that Mironnet
stayed in her employment.

Emotionally, Chanel seemed increasingly fragile. An insomniac, she went to bed at two in the morning and got up at six. She needed to follow a precise ritual in order to go to sleep: opening the windows wide, putting on pyjamas, wrapping her neck and hair in silk scarves. She needed an injection of Sedol (similar to Vicodin) or a suppository of Supponeryl (a sleeping medication) – something stronger than the pills she took to get herself through the day, supplied by her pharmacist in Lausanne. Although Marquand claimed that Chanel feared drugs, she depended on them to ease her psychological and physical pain. 'This is my life: a tranquilizer, a coffee, a tranquilizer, a coffee', she told Paul Morand.[25] 'At times your legend carries you along', she added, 'at other times you drown in it'.[26]

Marie-Hélène Arnaud in another Chanel suit, 1959.

10

Living Legend

When you are unhappy, attack.

Chanel, 1971[1]

Douglas Kirkland was a 27-year-old photo-journalist on assignment for *Look* magazine when he arrived in Paris in 1962 to do a story on Chanel. At the magazine, there had been some debate about whether she even deserved a story, but the fashion editor, Patricia Coffin, prevailed. Although Chanel wanted a fashion spread, the magazine decided to focus the article on *her*; despite misgivings, hungry for publicity as she was, she conceded but insisted on approving prints of Kirkland's photographs. At first, he found her intimidating: one morning, he remembered, he turned a corner in the salon and unexpectedly found himself face-to-face with her. 'She looked straight at me and said, "Salut". I froze', he said, unsure of his French and unaware that she had spent considerable time in England. 'After a beat, in her low voice, she said in perfect English, "I just said hello to you."'[2] Gradually, Kirkland became more at ease with her and she began to treat him warmly – 'as the son she never had', he thought, 'or some distant lover from her past'.[3]

At work, surrounded by assistants, Chanel performed for the camera, a diva in the atelier, lighting filter cigarettes with a 1925 Dunhill lighter that she said was a gift – likely from the Duke of Westminster. She enacted a different role at openings, when she retreated to the top of the stairs as mannequins paraded, and then received accolades at a champagne reception in the main dressing room, surrounded by customers that included – in early August 1962 – Claude Pompidou (wife of the French Prime Minister), the actress Rachel Roberts, Princess Lee Radziwill, Art Buchwald and many newspaper and magazine editors and illustrators.

By the end of the visit, Chanel asked Kirkland to lunch at her apartment one Saturday afternoon and to accompany her to Versailles. By the time lunch was over, Chanel had invited her young friend to vacation with her in Switzerland, where she promised him a chance to take more pictures. Versailles, though, was their immediate destination; after a few hours there, it began to rain, and Kirkland offered Chanel his raincoat. 'As our time was ending', he recalled,

> I looked back in the graying light and saw her small figure in the distance. I asked myself, 'How could such a small individual command such power?' I raised my camera quietly and made one final photo, which is my lasting vision of Coco Chanel.[4]

Despite Kirkland's apparent affection and respect for his subject, Chanel was unhappy with the article that *Look* published on 23 October 1962. She vented her anger at Patricia Coffin, who decided, ultimately, that Chanel would never be pleased with anything written about her, by anyone. And yet she wanted to be written about, noticed and respected by a world that seemed to be forgetting her. A few years after her comeback, she pinned her hopes on Broadway.

'I'd been fascinated with Chanel since I was ten', producer Frederick Brisson said, explaining his decision to mount a story of her life. 'I was fascinated by this woman who cut her hair, smoked in public, wore pants.'[5] Depending on whose version of events one believes, Brisson – already a producer of the hugely successful musicals *The Pajama Game* (1954) and *Damn Yankees*

(1955) – tried to get Chanel to agree to the production as early as 1954, pleading his case each time he visited her in Paris. But she refused, just as she reputedly refused Louis B. Mayer when he had tried to buy the rights to her life story in the late 1930s. She was afraid of exposure, afraid that she would not be able to control her carefully honed myth. 'People with a legend end up being like their legend', she once told Dalí, 'so as to reinforce their own celebrity'.[6] But in 1957, she invited Brisson and his wife, Rosalind Russell, to dinner and finally agreed.[7] Claude Delay says she changed her mind because she trusted Americans, but it seems likely that she saw this play as desperately needed publicity. A Broadway show – and, she hoped, an international tour and a film – would enhance her name.

During the initial discussions, Chanel suggested Cocteau as a possible scriptwriter – a man she thought she could manipulate, after all, because he was indebted to her. But Brisson, wisely enough, wanted Alan Jay Lerner, whose book for *My Fair Lady* had earned him enormous acclaim.[8] Chanel had not much liked *My Fair Lady* because of costumes that she considered inauthentic; she insisted that she was no 'fair lady' and likened herself instead to Professor Higgins – and Pygmalion. Still, she thought Lerner was refined enough to transform her life into a musical. Lerner came to the project shortly after *Camelot* opened on Broadway in 1960; and after Richard Rogers dropped out of consideration to write the music, André Previn signed on for his Broadway debut instead.

Even with Chanel's consent, however, no contract was signed for several years, during which time Brisson discovered that the legal rights to anything with the Chanel name on it were controlled by Pierre Wertheimer. The House of Chanel, Wertheimer told Brisson, was decidedly not interested in a Broadway show, which could do nothing but cheapen the brand. In contrast to her earlier dealings with Wertheimer, this time Chanel surrounded herself with advisers who took the lead in negotiating: her lawyers René de Chambrun and Edouard de Segonzac, and her friend Hervé Mille. After months of correspondence and haggling, finally a fourteen-page contract emerged that gave Brisson the right to proceed, but only if he were to agree to the many stipulations: the script could include only those events from Chanel's life that she approved; no use of the name Chanel could be in the libretto, other than to identify the character and the name of her shop; the portrayal would do nothing to harm Chanel's stature and prestige; and no one in the play would represent Wertheimer or anyone else at Chanel, Inc. Furthermore, if the play eventually became a film, it had to be made by a major producer and distributed by a major distributor; and if it was purchased by television, then it must be on a national network with no advertisements by any company whose products competed with Chanel, Inc. Chanel herself kept the rights to approve the final libretto and, she thought, the choice of the actress who would portray her.

The libretto was long in coming. 'Mlle Chanel is a fascinating person', Lerner said, 'but to most Americans she is just a brand of perfume. It will be like telling the public there is a Mr Buick – we'll have to bring the product to life.'[9] But bringing Chanel to life, with restrictions on what Lerner could use, proved difficult. Research materials included an entry on Chanel in *Current Biography* for 1954 and several magazine articles. All these sources repeated familiar anecdotes about Chanel's life: her abandonment by her loving father, her rich and famous lovers, her devotion to work, her revolution in liberating women from nineteenth-century bustles, corsets and furbelows. The play was to begin with Chanel's return to the fashion business in 1954; unfortunately, as Lerner portrayed her in early drafts, she came across as a bitter, garrulous old woman. Even as late as 1967, after many rewrites, Brisson's readers found the script weak, the dialogue stilted and the central character unsympathetic. Who would care whether she returned to her business or not? The play needed a central love story, one reader advised; without it, the plot dragged.

Still, Lerner kept rewriting and Brisson moved forward. Paramount Pictures, in exchange for rights to film the story, backed the production at a cost of £560,000 – making it the most expensive Broadway show in history. Cecil Beaton, designer for *My Fair Lady*, signed on to work on the costumes and scenery. His 253 costumes alone cost £93,000. Although he designed only two sets, these were elaborate and mechanically intricate – one replicated the mirrored, beige-carpeted stairway in Chanel's salon.

The show did not yet have a star but Chanel suggested several possibilities: Elizabeth Taylor, for one, or Julie Christie; but Brisson firmly insisted that the decision was his, despite Chanel's ever-changing opinions. 'You know how it goes', he told a reporter, 'she sees a different movie with a different actress and changes her mind every week.'[10] His first choice was Audrey Hepburn, whose petite slenderness made her most physically like Chanel, and whose success as Eliza Doolittle in *My Fair Lady* had made her one of Broadway's most sought after stars. In the spring of 1963, Brisson begged her to meet with Chanel while she was in France filming *Paris When it Sizzles* and *Charade*. But Hepburn – who had expressed mild interest in the role the year before – found no time to visit with Chanel; and besides, she told Brisson, she really did not feel she was right for the part. Once Hepburn declined, Rosalind Russell assumed that the role would be hers: 'I read the script Monday night and told my husband Tuesday morning that I would do the part.'[11]

In 1966, Brisson recalled, Lerner sang a few numbers for Chanel, accompanied by Previn, and she read – and approved – the script in the form it took then. According to Claude Delay, however, Chanel never saw the script. 'She who was on guard against any indiscretion, any intrusion into her secret solitude, trusted Alan Lerner and Frederick Brisson to put *Coco* on Broadway, and didn't ask to see the script.'[12] If she did, then she knew that the plot showed her to be a woman angry that young designers were creating styles for young women; angry that fashion was – in her perception – dominated by gay men; angry at the Parisian press for thinking that she would fail. In the play, Chanel's father urges her to become a success, several rich lovers help set up her business, but in the end none of those lovers warms her life. Chanel dotes on a young, beautiful model and is distressed when the model decides to marry. Money and acclaim: these become the measures of her happiness, the refrain of one of the show's central songs. With so much perpetuating the legend that Chanel created, she may well have given the script her approval.

In February 1967, Brisson and Chanel gave a joint interview in Paris in which Brisson announced that the play was scheduled to open that autumn. But Previn was still working on the music, Brisson had not yet found a director or choreographer, and still the lead had not been cast. Both Lerner and Previn believed that Russell was not right for the role of a brittle, demanding couturière, and Lerner surreptitiously sent the script to the one actress he proclaimed was made for the part: Katharine Hepburn. At the same time that she received Lerner's flattering invitation to consider the part, Hepburn got a brief note from their mutual friend and confidante, Lillie Messinger, enthusiastically urging her to read the play.

The 62-year-old Hepburn was at a difficult moment in her life. Although she had just won two Academy Awards for her roles in *Guess Who's Coming to Dinner* (1967) and *The Lion in Winter* (1968), she was at a loss, grieving the death (only eight months earlier) of her companion Spencer Tracy. She was despondent and, she confessed to Lerner, was thinking of giving up acting entirely. Yet the prospect of a new challenge – singing and dancing were certainly new for her – and the prospect of returning to Broadway after fifteen years (her last performance was in George Bernard Shaw's *The Millionairess*) enticed her. Like Chanel, for Hepburn grief translated itself into an obsession to work and an obsessive need for adulation – the kind of adulation that could only be felt from an audience, in a theatre, night after night after night. She decided to return to the stage.

A few months after receiving the script from Lerner, she auditioned for Brisson, Russell and a few friends, talk-singing some Cole Porter numbers in the manner of Rex Harrison in *My Fair Lady*. Brisson remarked angrily that she sounded like Donald Duck, and Rosalind Russell – a veteran of musical comedy – agreed. But the couple could do nothing in the face of Hepburn's determination and Lerner's support. Show business newspapers and the general press perked up at a juicy scandal, feeding rumours that Rosalind Russell had been dropped, unwillingly and unhappily, from the role. Chanel added venom to the reports by claiming that Katharine Hepburn was her choice because she looked more like her than Russell, and she implied that Russell was too fat and not refined enough to play her – refinement being the attribute she most wanted from everyone involved. Although Russell resented Chanel's insinuations and certainly resented the underhanded way that Lerner approached Hepburn, her notes about the script indicate her own dissatisfaction: it lacked drama, the character of Coco seemed unmotivated and boring, the dialogue read too much like a string of quotations. Not playing Coco is likely to have been a relief. In the end, Brisson sent out a press release explaining that Russell had too many film commitments – starting with *The Unexpected Mrs Pollifax* – and could not take on a Broadway play.

Once she agreed to take the part, Hepburn – who had a reputation for admirable professionalism – suddenly became a diva: demanding and controlling. Among the benefits she required in her contract was approval of the director and choreographer. Since she was new to musical comedy, she insisted that she work with an experienced team: Jerome Robbins, Gower Champion, Herbert Ross, Michael Benthall or Mike Nichols were some of the names she first suggested. Her contract allowed her to submit a total of twelve names, provided she did so a year in advance of the start of rehearsals. She also stipulated that the producers had to pay for a singing coach, a secretary – her companion Phyllis Wilbourn filled that role – and a hairdresser. She wanted to decide on the theatre venue and on the leading man. If the play became a film, she would get £250,000 and 7.5 per cent of the profits.

She baulked at delays in starting rehearsals, angrily castigating Brisson and Lerner; when Brisson would not approve a trip to London for fittings with Beaton, she went anyway (with Wilbourn), travelling first class and charging the tickets to management; she kept Brisson waiting interminably while she decided how long she would appear in the show scheduled to open in the autumn: first it was until April, then June, then through the summer, then not, making it impossible for him to audition another actress to take over the role. When she saw the plans for publicity posters, she complained that her name was too small, Beaton's drawing of her unflattering and his signature too large. As far as the script was concerned, she was adamant about the casting for Noelle, the mannequin on whom Chanel dotes: the woman, Hepburn said, should not appear too masculine because it would fuel rumours of lesbianism which dogged both herself and Chanel throughout their lives. People were curious about Chanel's love life. Had Chanel and Misia been lovers? Was Maggie van Zuylen found in bed with her at La Pausa? Did she make advances to some of her young models, especially Marie-Hélène Arnaud? Did she have a tryst with Marlene Dietrich? Chanel answered these questions with a resounding 'No'.

As for rumours regarding Hepburn, although her biographer William Mann maintains that she and her constant companion Phyllis Wilbourn were not lovers, their relationship appeared to model that of Gertrude Stein and Alice B. Toklas, including Wilbourn's self-effacing role as facilitator in Hepburn's life. Hepburn had been linked with other women too, especially her long-time friend Laura Harding – who, Mann believes, was Hepburn's lover. For the part of Noelle, Hepburn apparently approved Gale Dixon, a 23-year-old actress with a sweet soprano voice, the epitome of an ingénue.

Eventually Michael Benthall directed and Michael Bennett choreographed, with Robert Emmett Dolan as music director. Once rehearsals finally began, Hepburn became even more infuriating. She insisted that the temperature in the theatre be kept to 15.5°C (59.9°F), which was uncomfortably cold for everyone else. Always first on stage and last to leave, she could work long hours without a break: 'The only time she panics is when she's left with nothing to do', Lerner said. The show, running two and a half hours, required her to be on stage for all but twelve minutes, but she was not at all daunted. 'I think I'm feisty', she said.[13] Hard as she worked in rehearsal, she became frustrated easily and needed constant praise. It's no wonder that after Hepburn visited Chanel in Paris she went away sure of their affinity. 'We're not so different', she remarked to her confidant Garson Kanin.[14]

Chanel intended to be on hand for the opening at the Mark Hellinger Theatre on 18 December 1969, remembering, no doubt, the effusive reception she had received in New York during her trips there decades before. She had a white sequinned dress made for the event, but put off buying her ticket to the States. A week before the opening, Delay went to her apartment at the Ritz – taking with her Maurice Sachs's *Witches Sabbath*, which Chanel wanted to reread – and found a physician just leaving: Chanel's right hand was paralysed. At the American Hospital in Neuilly, she was told that it would take three months before she would regain use of her hand, a prospect that dismayed her. When Serge Lifar told her he knew a Swedish healer, she demanded that he send for him. 'The healer came to the Ritz', Delay said, 'sang the whole of *Pagliacci* in the Psyche salon, and kissed her hand but didn't bring it back to life'.[15] She decided to stay in Paris.

After 40 previews and no out-of-town try out, the show drew the strongest advanced sales ever seen on Broadway. *Coco*, newspapers and magazines reported, was 'the most anticipated opening' of the season, and the first night audience burst with celebrities: among them Douglas Fairbanks Jr, Otto Preminger, Danny Kaye, Martha Graham, Previn's pregnant fiancée Mia Farrow, Lauren Bacall, Ruth Gordon and Lee Radziwill. Some women wore Chanel; others wore one of her competitors – including James Galanos, who was on hand wearing a Dior coat. The clothes in the lobby, wrote Bernadine Morris, fashion reporter for the *New York Times*, were as glamorous as those Beaton made for the stage.[16]

Yet for all the excitement and glitz, the play itself disappointed nearly all reviewers. Clive Barnes, writing in the *New York Times*, admitted that he had had no idea who or what 'Coco' was – maybe, he wondered, it was the name of a low-calorie chocolate drink? He thought the script was boring, the music 'so unmemorable as to be uncriticizable' and the sets 'ugly' and 'nondescript'. But Hepburn, he exulted, was 'a blithe spirit, a vital flame'. 'Her singing voice is unique', he wrote, 'a neat mixture of faith, love and laryngitis, unforgettable, unbelievable and delightful'.[17] Richard Watts, critic for the *New York Post*, agreed, calling the show 'surprisingly dull . . . seriously handicapped by an inferior book and a very minor score'.[18] Still, he too – like John Chapman in the *Daily News* – raved about Hepburn's performance, which received ovations every night, applause that she craved. Despite reviews, ticket sales were brisk and Hepburn was nominated for a Tony Award – losing, finally, to Lauren Bacall for *Applause*.

If Hepburn had sounded like a duck in her earlier impromptu performance for Lerner and Brisson, by the time the show opened she had perfected her attack on the music. Performing six out of thirteen songs in the show, she belted out lyrics in a voice that captured Chanel's grittiness and never attempted to emulate a French accent. Hepburn's diction was what it always was: an amalgam of Connecticut and Philadelphia Main Line. With passion and conviction, her Coco protested against anyone who said that her fame was over, that she could never make a successful comeback. 'The Money Rings Out Like Freedom', she proclaimed. With American department stores eager for her designs, it just was not true that 'The World Belongs to the Young'. Chanel sent Hepburn a telegram of congratulations. Privately, she hoped Broadway was only the first stop on the dissemination of her legendary tale. She hoped Hepburn would take the show – *Chanel*'s show – on the road, across America and Europe.

Despite the rousing song, Chanel increasingly saw that the fashion world *did* belong to the young. She was adamant in criticizing current fashion, even when it was more conventional than the mini-skirts and slacks that she so despised. One of the targets of her wrath was Jacqueline Kennedy, whom Chanel castigated as having 'horrible taste and she's responsible for spreading it all over America'. A short-skirted white Courrèges dress seemed to her particularly reprehensible. Other designers quickly leapt to Kennedy's defence. 'Just look at Mrs Kennedy and look at Chanel', said Oleg Cassini, one of Kennedy's favourite designers: 'I'm afraid that there comes a time when life passes you by and leaves you with nothing but your memories of the ability to attack other people. Great as Chanel has been, she's had it, as least as far as reasoning and good taste.' Twenty-four-year-old Betsey Johnson was more generous: 'I really think Chanel was fabulous', she said, 'and for the older woman, she's still fabulous . . . But fashion for young people is the expression of their lives, and Chanel just isn't in her twenties.'[19]

In 1967, Saks Fifth Avenue – one of her stalwart customers – stopped buying from her and she was furious. Looking for new inspiration, she suddenly turned to one of her newest friends, Bettina Graziani. One day, with a mouthful of pins, she turned to Bettina and said, unexpectedly: 'I want to do a collection on you.' Among the most well-paid fashion models of the 1940s and '50s, Bettina (born Simone Micheline Bodin) worked for Lucien Lelong,

Jacques Fath and Hubert de Givenchy before she gave up modelling in 1955 – just as Chanel was making her comeback. As a muse to Fath and Givenchy, Bettina had an experienced eye for tailoring, and had much respect for Chanel as a genius who paid attention to an outfit's every detail. Dresses were lined with *peau de soie*; jackets were weighted with chains so they would not lose their shape, no matter how a woman moved. At fittings, Chanel had models lift their arms over their heads so that armholes could allow for movement, and a jacket or dress would still hang perfectly.[20]

Never part of Chanel's exclusive *cabine*, as the fiancée of Prince Aly Khan, Bettina sometimes became a customer. Bettina had the air of a gamine – petite, fresh-faced, freckled – and a svelte figure perfect for Chanel's designs. Although Chanel was twice Bettina's age, she befriended her, perhaps finding an affinity in their backgrounds – Bettina, like Chanel, escaped a provincial upbringing to come to Paris, and like Chanel, she had been devastated by the loss of her lover when Prince Aly Khan was killed in a car crash only a few years after their engagement. Whatever the reason, Chanel felt inspired by the younger woman. When Bettina needed a costume for an 'India' ball at Hotel Lombard in the 1960s, Chanel made not one but two costumes, and instructed Bettina to change during the ball. While working on the costumes, Chanel needed to be hospitalized briefly at the American Hospital, so Bettina found herself being fitted in the hospital room.

At the showing of 'her' collection, Bettina caused a stir among the press in attendance who celebrated her return. Chanel – seated at the top of the mirrored staircase – became incensed, storming out because it was Bettina and not Chanel herself who was applauded. It was a shock to Bettina but by then she was well aware of Chanel's loneliness and isolation, her unprovoked rages. Mercilessly critical of other people, she could count only on a few trusted and patient friends: journalist Jacques Chazot (with whom she would go to flea markets) and Hervé Mille.

By the late 1960s, many who visited her were struck by how old she looked and how angry she seemed. Cecil Beaton, who saw her in 1970, gave a typical report: 'Her hair the blackest of dyed wool, without shape or gloss, her eyes made up underneath to look like an aged dog, a dreadful white felt hat . . . The old gypsy at once turned on her conversation machine and allowed me no opportunity to interject. She talked as usual of the horrors of present-day life.' Her rings, some looking like gold wedding bands, slipped on her thin fingers. One sapphire ring fell off and was lost. 'It didn't love me and it's gone – I don't care', she said.[21] She wore black boots to hide her swollen ankles. Her appearance was so unlike the attractive woman she had been 30 years before when no one, Beaton said, could match her allure.

'Everyone except her was at fault', Beaton recalled. Her conversation centred only on the negative, particularly gossip about other women – like Maggie Van Zuylen, once a close friend – who according to Chanel did nothing with their lives but play bridge. She said Maggie had been too fat all her life and then proceeded to criticize all fat people. In a scene echoed by everyone who spent time with Chanel, she kept talking incessantly, even following Beaton as he tried to leave. 'She fought like a dragon to keep the conversation going so that I could not say goodbye', he remembered.[22] Even when he was on the landing, down the stairs, she followed. 'The rough voice still went on. Then you blew a kiss. She knew now that loneliness again faced her. She smiled a goodbye, the mouth stretched in a grimace, but from a distance that grimace worked. It contained the old allure.' Although Beaton could be as catty as Chanel ever was, he conceded that she was an exceptional – and exceptionally sexy – woman,

> unfeminine in character but totally feminine in her attitudes to enticement . . . She had an 'eye' to quality and proportion that was unbeatable. She had daring, freshness, authority,

conviction. She had genius and all her faults must be forgiven for that one reason.[23]

Horst, visiting in 1963, recalled the apartment looking like a museum, filled with hugely valuable objects, including gold knives and forks. He noticed that vermeil dressing-table sets of brushes, bottles and powder boxes were still in her bathroom, but she had had their engraved ducal coronets removed, perhaps – as Marquand had noted – in a gesture of revising her life story.[24] Marcel Haedrich thought the apartment looked like Ali Baba's cave. The objects, though, had far greater value to Chanel than their monetary worth; they were precious relics from her life: ears of gilded wheat, a single chaff painted on black by Dalí, rows of scissors on her dressing-table, a Russian virgin hanging over her bed at the Ritz, crystal balls on a coffee table, images of lions everywhere. On a side table, there was a bronze hand of Delay by sculptor Diego Giacometti (younger brother of Alberto, who had been treated by Delay's husband, a prominent hand surgeon).

Surrounded by reminders of the past, Chanel looked back with nostalgia and regret. 'Her nostalgia was for tenderness', Delay wrote, which Chanel defined as 'strength watching over you'.[25] Her regret, as always, was over not being loved. 'My life is a failure. Don't you think it's a failure, to work as I work, under this lamp?' she asked Delay. 'I've cried a lot.' Having lost so many lovers, she had taken refuge, she said, 'in dresses and coats'.[26] But that refuge did not protect her; success felt hollow and the version of her life that others repeated with admiration – the glittering anecdotes, the witty maxims – was of no comfort to her. 'Lie if you must', she told Joseph Barry, 'but never in detail, or to yourself'.[27]

Looking in a mirror, she told Paul Morand,

I see myself with my two menacing arched eyebrows, my nostrils that are as wide as those of a mare, my hair that is blacker than the devil, my mouth that is like a crevice out of which pours a heart that is irritable but unselfish; crowning all that, a great knot of schoolgirl's hair set above the troubled face of a woman who spent too much time at school! My dark, gipsy-like skin that makes my teeth and my pearls look twice as white; my body, as dry as a vine-stock without grapes; my worker's hands with cabochons that resemble an imitation American knuckle-duster.

The hardness of the mirror reflects my own hardness back to me; it's a struggle between it and me: it expresses what is peculiar to myself, a person who is efficient, optimistic, passionate, realistic, combative, mocking and incredulous, and who feels her Frenchness.[28]

She played out her efficiency and passion every working day, reigning at the rue Cambon, even though she could no longer hold scissors to cut. But weekends could be desolate. On Sundays she sometimes walked in the cemetery of Père Lachaise or stayed home alone. Sometimes Delay would have lunch with her; she noticed that Chanel had become obsessed with cleanliness. At the Ritz, she sent knives and forks back, saying they were not clean; when she was in the hospital, she complained that nothing was clean – she sent glasses back to be washed.

Evenings, too, were unbearably lonely for her, and she watched television late into the night. 'I often found her, touching in her solitude, sitting at her dressing-table and staring out blankly into the garden', Delay recalled. 'Slender still in her shift, she would suddenly appear to me with the wrinkles of all the years above her bare arms . . . Arms which hadn't embraced. Her eyebrows not drawn, thin in her silk pyjamas, bows of brown ribbon over her fringe, she was alone with her eighteen-year old heart. What she called her infantilism.'[29] Sleeping had become more of a problem. Even with sedatives, she was beset by nightmares and episodes of sleepwalking. She sometimes took scissors and attacked the

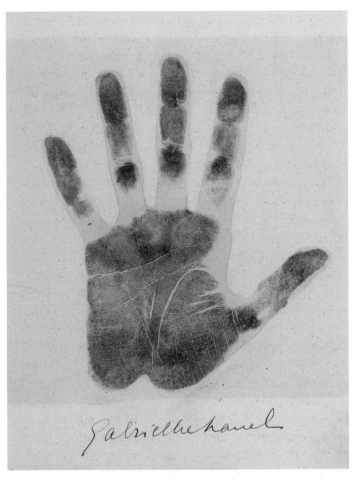

Imprint of Chanel's hand, 1939.

bedclothes to try to make an outfit; sometimes she washed her hands, repeatedly rinsing her fingertips. She asked to be tied down to the bed.

She hoped, she said, to die at work. But on Sunday night, on 10 January 1971, she suddenly could not breathe, and she tried – but failed – to give herself an injection. Her maid, rushing in to help, found her in a state of panic. By the time the hotel physician arrived, she was dead.

'A woman who's not loved is no woman. Whatever her age', she had said. 'A woman who's not loved is a woman that's lost. The only thing for her to do is die.'[30]

A memorial service at L'Église de la Madeleine was a reunion of Paris fashion stars: Yves Saint-Laurent, Guy Laroche, Pierre Balmain, Marc Bohan, Cristóbal Balenciaga all filed into the church, along with many of Chanel's mannequins, all wearing coats that she had designed. Dalí was there too, as were Hervé Mille, Lilou Marquand and François Mironnet. Claude Delay came with her husband; Edmonde Charles-Roux and Jacques Chazot also attended. These were among the hundreds – reports said 2,000 – who filled the church for the Latin Mass. Flowers were everywhere: Freddie Brisson and his wife Rosalind Russell sent white azaleas; Visconti, a wreath of red roses and camellias; Mironnet, a cross of white flowers. As the coffin was slipped into a hearse for the trip to Lausanne where Chanel would be buried, rumours began to fly: Charles-Roux, it was said, had finished a revealing biography of Chanel that would be published shortly now that the designer was dead. An assistant, it was said, had slipped a few rings from her fingers and pocketed them. Mironnet, it was said, claimed that Chanel had promised him a million dollars. And, of course, amid the rumours, there was one crucial question: would the House of Chanel continue?

Of course, it did. The Wertheimers were still in control, and with the death of Pierre in 1965, his son Jacques took over. The collection that Chanel had readied for the next showing was finished, and if the house lagged a bit for the next three years, once Jacques' son Alain took over in 1974, he infused a new spirit in the company. With a new advertising campaign for perfumes and cosmetics, and the opening of 40 Chanel boutiques throughout the world, sales revived.

In 1983, German-born Karl Lagerfeld was appointed as head of design for the House of Chanel. Fifteen years of age when he arrived in Paris with his mother and seventeen when he won a fashion award for a coat design, Lagerfeld had worked for both Pierre Balmain and Jean Patou before he decided to move to ready-to-wear houses, snubbing the world of *haute couture* as too rarefied. But ready-to-wear failed to sustain his interest and he left fashion completely for a while, deciding to study art instead. Still, fashion drew him back, and he designed for Fendi and Chloé. Like Chanel, he has a reputation as a hard and tireless worker; unlike Chanel, he draws, and his designs reveal both grace and verve. Although his early collections paid homage to Chanel's iconic styles, he soon developed his own look that was more playful and street-smart. 'I took her code, her language and mixed it all up', he said.[31] Jeans, bikers' jackets, 10-cm (4-in.) heels and sequins characterize many of Lagerfeld's creations for the House of Chanel.

Because Chanel is a privately held company, financial analysts can only estimate its worth. A recent analysis compared the house to another privately held European brand, Hermès, and added to a valuation of the fashion revenue an estimate of the perfume and cosmetics business. Even during periods of recession throughout the world, Chanel seems to have held its value. 'Take one C, interlock it with another C, and what you have is priceless', said a chief analyst at a market research company. With a fashion business worth £3 billion to almost £5 billion, future earning potential of £1–2 billion

Karl Lagerfeld's playful version of a Chanel suit for the 2011 Spring/ Summer Ready-to Wear collection.

as the economy strengthens, and a perfume and cosmetics business worth £2–2.5 billion, the company achieved a valuation of £6 to nearly £9 billion in 2008, making it one of the strongest fashion houses in the world.[32]

In 1997, 75 years after the creation of Chanel No. 5, a new advertising campaign linking Chanel with Andy Warhol (who used the No. 5 bottle in a series of works) gave the perfume a younger image among buyers who associated the scent with their mothers' fashions. The campaign generated a 20–30 per cent surge in sales, reviving a perfume whose appeal seems imperishable. Recently, two films about Chanel were released: *Coco avant Chanel* starring Audrey Tautou (2009), and *Coco and Igor* starring Anna Mouglalis (2009). Tautou, besides appearing as the young Chanel in the film, also was featured in romantic television and print advertisements for Chanel No. 5.

'Couturières, like actresses, have generally but a fugitive success', Chanel's friend Maurice Sachs once wrote; 'at their death they leave no living trace, and sometimes they are forgotten long before quitting this world – the former because fashion has turned from them, the latter because their applause has fallen into silence'.[33] Many famous couturiers have met that fate – Patou, Paquin, Molyneux, Mainbocher and even Vionnet – but not Chanel: not her style, not her influence and not the woman that she so astoundingly was.

References

Introduction

1 Quoted in Salvador Dalí, *The Unspeakable Confessions of Salvador Dalí*, trans. Harold J. Salemson (New York, 1976), p. 210.
2 Claude Delay, *Chanel Solitaire*, trans. Barbara Bray (New York, 1974), p. 58.
3 *Vogue* (1 April 1919), p. 48.
4 Joseph Barry, 'An Interview with Chanel', *McCall's* (November 1965), p. 170.
5 John Fairchild, *The Fashionable Savages* (New York, 1965), pp. 42–3.
6 'A Designing Designer', *The Washington Post* (21 June 1936), p. B6.
7 Joseph Barry, '"I Am on the Side of Women," Said My Friend Chanel', *Smithsonian* (May 1971), p. 29.
8 Ibid., p.35.
9 Ibid., pp. 142, 145, 147.
10 Valerie Steele, 'Chanel: "L'Élégance, C'est Moi"', *Women of Fashion: Twentieth-Century Designers* (New York, 1991), p. 53.

1 A Small Dark Girl

1 Chanel to Joseph Barry, 'An Interview with Chanel', *McCall's* (November 1965), p. 174.
2 Louise de Vilmorin, *Mémoires de Coco* (Paris, 1999), p. 17.
3 Bettina Ballard, *In My Fashion* (New York, 1960), pp. 50–51.
4 Pierre Galante, *Mademoiselle Chanel*, trans. Eileen Geist and Jessie Wood (Chicago, IL, 1973), p. 75.

5   Barry, 'An Interview with Chanel', p. 170.

6   Ibid., p. 170.

7   Paul Morand, *The Allure of Chanel* [1976], trans. Euan Cameron (London, 2008), p. 39.

8   'The Strong Ones', *The New Yorker* (28 September 1957), p. 34.

9   Morand, *The Allure of Chanel*, p. 23.

10   Claude Delay, *Chanel Solitaire*, trans. Barbara Bray (New York, 1974), p. 184.

11   Ibid., p. 16.

12   Vilmorin, *Mémoires de Coco*, p. 33. Quoted in 'Maximes and Sentences', French *Vogue* (September 1938), pp. 56–7.

13   Marcel Haedrich, *Coco Chanel: Her Life, her Secrets*, trans. Charles Lam Markmann (Boston, MA, 1972) p. 67.

14   Morand, *The Allure of Chanel*, p. 54.

15   Ibid., p. 34.

16   Delay, *Chanel Solitaire*, p. 184.

17   Morand, *The Allure of Chanel*, p. 39.

18   Robert Phelps, ed., *Professional Secrets: An Autobiography of Jean Cocteau*, trans. Richard Howard (New York, 1970), p. 53.

19   Ibid., p. 54.

20   Quoted in Stephen Walsh, *Stravinsky, A Creative Spring: Russia and France, 1882–1934* (New York, 1999), p. 120.

21   Morand, *The Allure of Chanel*, p. 84.

2   Boaters

1   Chanel, 'Secrets de jeunesse', *Marie Claire* (5 November 1937), p. 33.

2   'Say Americans Ruin Deauville', *New York Times* (17 August 1913), p. 1.

3   'Deauville Sands Blaze With Jewels', *New York Times* (24 August 1913), p. 1.

4   'What the Well-Dressed Woman is Wearing', *New York Times* (29 September 1912), p. SM16.

5   'New Fashions not Greatly Different from Those of Spring', *New York Times* (7 September 1913), p. SM12.

6   'Hands in Pockets New Paris Mode', *New York Times* (6 October 1913), p. 3.

7   Quoted in Brenda Polan and Roger Tredre, *The Great Fashion*

Designers (Oxford, 2009), p. 21.

8   *Women's Wear Daily* (27 July 1914).

9   *Vogue* (1 February 1916), p. 37.

10 Quoted in Valerie Steele, 'Chanel: "L'Élégance, C'est Moi"', *Women of Fashion: Twentieth-Century Designers* (New York, 1991), p. 44.

11 *Vogue* (15 January 1917), p. 32.

12 *Vogue* (15 May 1917), p. 48.

13 *Vogue* (1 August 1918), p. 40; *New York Times* (2 February 1919). The German Shepherd dog Rin Tin Tin derives its name from the male mascot; the first Rin Tin Tin was discovered abandoned in Paris among a litter found by an American officer.

14 *Vogue* (15 March 1919), p. 35.

15 Maurice Sachs, *The Decade of Illusion: Paris, 1918–1928*, trans. Gladys Matthews Sachs (New York, 1933), pp. 158–9.

16 Quoted in Pierre Galante, *Mademoiselle Chanel*, trans. Eileen Geist and Jessie Wood (Chicago, IL, 1973), p. 42.

17 Paul Morand, *Venices* [1971], trans. Euan Cameron (London, 2002), pp. 121–2.

18 Horst P. Horst, *Salute to the Thirties* (New York, 1971), p. 163.

19 Ibid., p. 12.

20 Mme Henri Bernstein, quoted in Galante, *Mademoiselle Chanel*, p. 83.

21 Claude Delay, *Chanel Solitaire*, trans. Barbara Bray (New York, 1974), p. 184.

22 Axel Madsen, *Chanel: A Woman of her Own* (New York, 1990), p. 89.

23 Paul Morand, *The Allure of Chanel* [1976], trans. Euan Cameron (London, 2008), p. 38.

24 Ibid., p. 66.

3 *À la folie*

1   Maurice Sachs, *The Decade of Illusion: Paris, 1918–1928*, trans. Gladys Matthews Sachs (New York, 1933), p. 155.

2   Maurice Sachs, *Witches' Sabbath* [1960], trans. Richard Howard (New York, 1964), pp. 69–70.

3   *Vogue* (1 August 1920), p. 35.

4   *Women's Wear Daily* (1 February 1924).

5 *Woman's Wear Daily* (24 February 1922).

6 *Woman's Wear Daily* (23 February 1923).

7 Jean Cocteau, 'From Worth to Alix', *Harper's Bazaar* (March 1937), p. 147.

8 'A Perfect Wardrobe for the Sportswoman', *Vogue* (15 May 1923), p. 53.

9 Edna Woolman Chase and Ilka Chase, *Always in Vogue* (London, 1954), p. 183.

10 *Vogue* (15 May 1923), p. 41; French *Vogue* (1 May 1923), p. 22.

11 French *Vogue* (1 June 1925), p. 23.

12 'The Importance of the Corset Today', *Vogue* (15 September 1923), p. 94.

13 Joseph Barry, 'An Interview with Chanel', *McCall's* (November 1965), p. 170.

14 Paul Morand, *The Allure of Chanel* [1976], trans. Euan Cameron (London, 2008), pp. 127, 129.

15 Charles M. Joseph, *Stravinsky Inside Out* (New Haven, CT, 2001), p. 74.

16 Consuelo Vanderbilt Balsan, *The Glitter and the Gold* (New York, 1952), p. 200.

17 *Time* (13 August 1928).

18 Quoted in André Breton, *Conversations: The Autobiography of Surrealism*, trans. Mark Polizzotti (New York, 1993), p. 30.

19 Edmonde Charles-Roux, *Chanel: Her Life, her World, and the Woman Behind the Legend she herself Created*, trans. Nancy Amphoux (New York, 1975), p. 213.

20 Claude Delay, *Chanel Solitaire*, trans. Barbara Bray (New York, 1974), p. 135.

21 Ibid., p. 30.

22 Morand, *The Allure of Chanel*, p. 155

23 Ibid., p. 148.

24 Elizabeth Hawes, *Fashion is Spinach* (New York, 1938), pp. 60–61.

25 Ibid., p. 112.

26 Paul Padgette, ed., *The Dance Writings of Carl Van Vechten* (New York, 1974), p. 60.

27 Marie, Grand Duchess of Russia, *A Princess in Exile* (New York, 1932), pp. 173–4.

28 Morand, *The Allure of Chanel*, p. 81.

29 'Baron de Meyer Attends the Openings', *Harper's Bazaar* (April 1926), p. 118.

4 Double C

1 Claude Delay, *Chanel Solitaire*, trans. Barbara Bray (New York, 1974), p. 158

2 Quoted in Pierre Galante, *Mademoiselle Chanel*, trans. Eileen Geist and Jessie Wood (Chicago, IL, 1973), p. 39.

3 Ibid., p. 240.

4 Delay, *Chanel Solitaire*, p. 66.

5 Diana Crane, *Fashion and its Social Agendas: Class, Gender, and Identity in Clothing* (Chicago, IL, 2000), p. 151.

6 Quoted in Galante, *Mademoiselle Chanel*, p. 80.

7 Ibid., p. 87.

8 Delay, *Chanel Solitaire*, p. 86.

9 Galante, *Mademoiselle Chanel*, p. 85.

10 No. 5 Carte d'identité, Maison Chanel.

11 Delay, *Chanel Solitaire*, p. 131.

12 Marcel Haedrich, *Coco Chanel: Her Life, her Secrets*, trans. Charles Lam Markmann (Boston, MA, 1972), p. 103.

13 Ibid., p. 56.

14 Delay, *Chanel Solitaire*, p. 86.

15 Robert Phelps, ed., *Professional Secrets: An Autobiography of Jean Cocteau*, trans. Richard Howard (New York, 1970), pp. 50–51.

16 Quoted in Frank W. D. Ries, *The Dance Theatre of Jean Cocteau* (Ann Arbor, MI, 1986), p. 92.

17 William Wiser, *The Crazy Years: Paris in the Twenties* (New York, 1983), p. 77.

18 Serge Lifar, *My Life*, trans. James Holman Mason (New York, 1970), p. 35.

19 Jacques Lipchitz, *My Life in Sculpture* (New York, 1972), pp. 63, 67.

5 Sporting Life

1 Martin Gilbert, *Winston S. Churchill*, vol. V: *Companion, Part I, 1922–1929* (London, 1979), p. 1059.

2 Loelia Ponsonby, *Grace and Favour: The Memoirs of Loelia, Duchess of Westminster* (New York, 1961) p. 181.

3 Leslie Field, *Bendor: The Golden Duke of Westminster* (London, 1983), p. 163.

4   Joseph Barry, 'An Interview with Chanel', *McCall's* (November 1965), p. 173.
5   Stella Margetson, *The Long Party: High Society in the Twenties and Thirties* (Farnborough, Hampshire, 1974), p. 71.
6   Paul Morand, *The Allure of Chanel* [1976], trans. Euan Cameron (London, 2008) pp. 160, 163.
7   Ponsonby, *Grace and Favour*, p. 185.
8   *New York Times* (18 November 1928), p. 9; (9 February 1930), p. E3.
9   *Harper's Bazaar* (April 1926), pp. 118, 121.
10 French *Vogue* (1 June 1927).
11 Gilbert, *Winston S. Churchill*, Churchill to Clementine, January 1927, pp. 928–9.
12 Gilbert, *Winston S. Churchill*, Churchill to Clementine, 1 October 1927, p. 1059.
13 Ponsonby, *Grace and Favour*, pp. 217–8.
14 Field, *Bendor*, p. 205.
15 Morand, *The Allure of Chanel*, p. 84.
16 Ponsonby, *Grace and Favour*, p. 187.
17 Barry, 'An Interview with Chanel', p. 174.
18 Pierre Galante, *Mademoiselle Chanel*, trans. Eileen Geist and Jessie Wood (Chicago, IL, 1973), pp. 138, 139.
19 Ibid., p. 76.
20 Claude Delay, *Chanel Solitaire*, trans. Barbara Bray (New York, 1974), p. 125.
21 Quoted in Galante, *Mademoiselle Chanel*, p. 88.
22 Roderick W. Cameron, *The Golden Riviera* (London, 1978), pp. 48–9.
23 'Chanel Entertains at Brilliant Fete', *New York Times* (5 July 1931), p. 24.
24 'Notables Enliven Paris Yule Season', *New York Times* (13 December 1931), p. N7.

6 Diva

1   Colette, 'Chanel par Colette', *Bravo* (April 1930), p. 36.
2   'Haute Couture', *Time* (13 August 1934).
3   Elsa Schiaparelli, *Shocking Life* (New York, 1954), p. 64.

4　*New York Times* (3 February 1929), p. 120; (12 May 1929), p. x14; (9 June 1929), p. x10; (21 November 1929), p. 14.

5　Jean Cocteau, 'From Worth to Alix', *Harper's Bazaar* (March 1937), p. 172.

6　Jean Cocteau, *Past Tense: Diaries*, vol. i, trans. Richard Howard (New York, 1987), p. 146.

7　'Chanel Visits America', *New York Times* (8 March 1931), p. 121.

8　Janet Flanner, *Paris was Yesterday: 1925–1939* (New York, 1972), p. 77.

9　'Whence Come the Style Dicta for Mrs America?', *Washington Post* (8 May 1932), p. TG2.

10　Valentine Lawford, *Horst: His Work and his World* (New York, 1984), p. 109.

11　Horst P. Horst, *Salute to the Thirties* (New York, 1971), p. 12.

12　Flanner, *Paris was Yesterday*, pp. 86–7.

13　Gaia Servadio, *Luchino Visconti: A Biography* (New York, 1983), p. 42.

14　Paul Poiret, *King of Fashion: The Autobiography of Paul Poiret* [1931], trans. Stephen Haden (London, 2009), p. 48.

15　Paul Morand, *The Allure of Chanel* [1976], trans. Euan Cameron (London, 2008), pp. 110–11.

16　Ibid., pp. 111–12.

17　'Mlle Chanel to Wed Her Business Partner; Once Refused the Duke of Westminster', *New York Times* (19 November 1933), p. E3.

18　Morand, *The Allure of Chanel*, p. 109.

19　Ibid., p. 108.

20　Claude Delay, *Chanel Solitaire*, trans. Barbara Bray (New York, 1974), p. 153.

21　'Chanel Offers Her Shop to Workers to Run, Rather Than Make Contract She Can't Keep', *New York Times* (19 June 1936), p. 1.

7 History

1　Chanel, 'Secrets de jeunesse', *Marie Claire* (5 November 193), p. 33.

2　Virginia Pope, 'Paris Proposes and New York Accepts Super-Feminine Styles', *New York Times* (19 June 1938), p. 40.

3　*New York Times* (20 March 1931), p. 13.

4　Virginia Pope, 'The Season's Fashion High Spots Are Imported From Paris By New York', *New York Times* (4 April 1937), p. 94.

5 Virginia Pope, 'Paris Silhouettes Sensible This Year: Chanel and Alix Show Longer Skirts, Normal Shoulders and Waistlines', *New York Times* (3 August 1937), p. 25.

6 Virginia Pope, 'The New York Studios', *New York Times* (3 October 1937), p. 98.

7 'On the Isle of Capri', *Harper's Bazaar* (January 1939), p. 77.

8 Horst P. Horst, *Salute to the Thirties* (New York, 1971), p. 152.

9 Ibid., p. 12.

10 Ibid., p. 279.

11 Ibid., p. 156.

12 Chanel, 'Secrets de jeunesse', p. 33.

13 Alex-Ceslas Rzewuski, *La Double Tragedie de Misia Sert* (Paris, 2006), pp. 47–59.

14 Salvador Dalí, *The Secret Life of Salvador Dalí*, trans. Haakon M. Chevalier (New York, 1942), p. 382.

15 Valentine Lawford, *Horst: His Work and his World* (New York, 1984), p. 192.

16 Janet Flanner, 'Paris, Germany', *The New Yorker* (7 December 1940) p. 52; also see *The New Yorker Book of War Pieces* (New York, 1947), p. 78.

17 Hélène Gordon-Lazareff, 'The Paris Mode – A Mode of Defiance', *New York Times* (7 May 1944), p. SM11.

18 Catherine Mackenzie, 'Paris Fashions of the Thirties Provide a Footnote to History', *New York Times* (17 November 1940), p. 61.

8 Recluse

1 Paul Morand, *The Allure of Chanel* [1976], trans. Euan Cameron (London, 2008), p. 73.

2 Ibid., p. 73.

3 Quoted in Axel Madsen, *Chanel: A Woman of her Own* (New York, 1990), p. 257.

4 Michel Déon, 'Bagages Pour Vancouver', *Pages Françaises* (Paris, 1999), pp. 267–8.

5 Jean Cocteau, *Past Tense: Diaries*, vol. I, trans. Richard Howard (New York, 1987), p. 257.

6 Thomas F. Brady, 'Daring! Mad Love! Frantic!', *New York Times*

(11 July 1954), p. SM12.

7 Salvador Dalí, *The Unspeakable Confessions of Salvador Dalí, as Told to André Parinaud*, trans. Harold J. Salemson (New York, 1976), p. 211.

8 Louise de Vilmorin, *Mémoires de Coco* (Paris, 1999), p. 12.

9 Ibid., p. 21.

10 Madsen, *Chanel*, p. 274.

11 Cocteau, *Past Tense*, p. 51.

12 Quoted in Joseph Barry, 'Collections by Chanel', *McCall's* (June 1968), p. 54.

13 Pierre Galante, *Mademoiselle Chanel*, trans. Eileen Geist and Jessie Wood (Chicago, IL, 1973), p. 89.

14 Valentine Lawford, *Horst: His Work and his World* (New York, 1984), p. 323.

15 Elsa Schiaparelli, *Shocking Life* (New York, 1954), pp. 192–4.

16 Ibid., pp. 204–5.

9 Roped by Pearls

1 Paul Morand, *The Allure of Chanel* [1976], trans. Euan Cameron (London, 2008), p. 74.

2 Bettina Ballard, *In My Fashion* (New York, 1960), p. 58.

3 Quoted in Brigid Keenan, *Dior in Vogue* (New York, 1981), p. 56.

4 Christian Dior, *Talking about Fashion to Elie Rabourdin and Alice Chavanne*, trans. Eugenia Sheppard (New York, 1954), pp. 110–11.

5 Douglas Kirkland, *Coco Chanel: Three Weeks* (New York, 2008), p. 11.

6 Salvador Dalí, *The Unspeakable Confessions of Salvador Dalí, as Told to André Parinaud*, trans. Harold J. Salemson (New York, 1976), p. 211.

7 Djuna Barnes, 'Coco Talks', *Self* (August 1992), p. 168.

8 Jacques Chazot, Interview with Coco Chanel for the French TV programme *Dim Dam Dom* (1968).

9 Pierre Galante, *Mademoiselle Chanel*, trans. Eileen Geist and Jessie Wood (Chicago, IL, 1973), pp. 202–7.

10 Ballard, *In My Fashion*, p. 57.

11 'Feeneesh?', *Time* (15 February 1954).

12 Claude Delay, *Chanel Solitaire*, trans. Barbara Bray (New York, 1974), p. 61.

13 Virginia Pope, 'World of Fashion is Divided on Dior', *New York Times* (4 August 1954), p. 15; Nan Robertson, 'Designer Who Consults Fortune Teller Began an Empire with the "New Look"', *New York Times* (12 February 1957), p. 24.

14 Chanel gave her bag the nickname '2.55' because she launched it in February 1955.

15 *New York Times* (9 September 1957), p. 28.

16 *New York Times* (12 June 1957), p. 65.

17 *New Yorker* (28 September 1957), p. 35.

18 Quoted in Axel Madsen, *Chanel: A Woman of her Own* (New York, 1990), p. 298.

19 Lilou Marquand, *Chanel m'a dit* (Paris, 1990), p. 32.

20 Ibid., p. 44.

21 Ibid., p. 53.

22 Ibid., p. 108.

23 Delay, *Chanel Solitaire*, p. 146.

24 Ibid., p. 104.

25 Paul Morand, 'On Proust and Chanel', *Yale Review*, XCIV/2 (1 April 2006), p. 75.

26 Ibid., p. 82.

10 Living Legend

1 Chanel quoted in *Woman's Wear Daily* (1971), p. 9.

2 Douglas Kirkland, *Coco Chanel: Three Weeks* (New York, 2008), p. 11.

3 Ibid., p. 12.

4 Ibid., p. 13.

5 'Show Business: The Very Expensive Coco', *Time* (7 November 1969).

6 Salvador Dalí, *The Unspeakable Confessions of Salvador Dalí, as Told to André Parinaud*, trans. Harold J. Salemson (New York, 1976), p. 211.

7 Rosalind Russell and Chris Chase, *Life is a Banquet* (New York, 1977), pp. 180–81.

8 Unless otherwise noted, sources of information for the production of *Coco* come from the Frederick Brisson and Katharine Hepburn Papers at the Billy Rose Theatre Division of the New York Public Library for the Performing Arts.

9   Quoted in the *New York Herald Tribune* (20 April 1961).

10 'Chanel on the Styles of the Sixties: "It is a Lousy Time for Women"', *New York Times* (14 February 1967), p. 46.

11 'Rosalind Russell to Star in "Coco"', *New York Times* (27 September 1967), p. 43.

12 Claude Delay, *Chanel Solitaire*, trans. Barbara Bray (New York, 1974), p. 155.

13 'Show Business: The Very Expensive Coco' (7 November 1969).

14 Quoted in William J. Mann, *Kate, The Woman who was Hepburn* (New York, 2006), p. 443.

15 Ibid., p. 157.

16 'At "Coco", There Was a Fashion Show Both on Stage and Off', *New York Times* (19 December 1969), p. 59.

17 *New York Times* (19 December 1969), p. 66.

18 *New York Post* (19 December 1969), p. 30.

19 'Chanel in Dig at Mrs Kennedy's Taste', *New York Times* (29 July 1967), p. FS14.

20 Interview with Bettina Graziani (14 October 2009), Paris.

21 Delay, *Chanel Solitaire*, p. 139.

22 Cecil Beaton, *The Unexpurgated Beaton* (London, 2002), p. 115.

23 Ibid., pp. 123–4.

24 Valentine Lawford, *Horst: His Work and his World* (New York, 1984), p. 363.

25 Delay, *Chanel Solitaire*, p. 147.

26 Ibid., p. 143.

27 Joseph Barry, 'Collections by Chanel', *McCall's* (June 1968), p. 54.

28 Paul Morand, *The Allure of Chanel* [1976], trans. Euan Cameron (London, 2008), p. 143.

29 Ibid., p. 151.

30 Ibid., p. 147.

31 Brenda Polan and Roger Tredre, *The Great Fashion Designers* (Oxford, 2009), p. 134.

32 Willow Duttge, 'Buying Chanel (All of It)', *Condé Nast Portfolio* (June 2008).

33 Maurice Sachs, *The Decade of Illusion: Paris, 1918–1928*, trans. Gladys Matthews Sachs (New York, 1933), p. 153.

Select Bibliography

Ballard, Bettina, *In My Fashion* (New York, 1960)

Barry, Joseph, 'Portrait of Chanel No. 1', *New York Times* (23 August 1964)

——, 'An Interview with Chanel', *McCall's* (November 1965), pp. 121, 168–74

——, '"I Am on the Side of Women," Said My Friend Chanel', *Smithsonian* (May 1971), pp. 29–35

Bettina, *Bettina par Bettina* (Paris, 1964)

Bond, David, *Coco Chanel and Chanel* (London, 1994)

Bordo, Susan, *Unbearable Weight: Feminism, Western Culture, and the Body* (Berkeley, CA, 1993)

Bott, Danièle, *Chanel: Collections and Creations* (London, 2007)

Brady, James, *Superchic* (Boston, MA, 1974)

Cameron, Roderick W., *The Golden Riviera* (London, 1978)

Chanel, l'art comme univers, exh. cat., Pushkin State Museum of Fine Arts (Moscow, 2007)

Charles-Roux, Edmonde, *Chanel: Her Life, her World, and the Woman Behind the Legend she herself Created*, trans. Nancy Amphoux (New York, 1975)

——, *Chanel and her World: Friends, Fashion, and Fame*, trans. Daniel Wheeler (New York, 2005)

Chase, Edna Woolman, and Ilka Chase, *Always in Vogue* (London, 1954)

Cocteau, Jean, *Past Tense: Diaries*, vol. I, trans. Richard Howard (New York, 1987)

Crane, Diana, 'Postmodernism and the Avant-Garde: Stylistic Change in Fashion Design', *Modernism/Modernity*, IV/3 (1997), pp. 123–40

——, *Fashion and Its Social Agendas: Class, Gender, and Identity in Clothing* (Chicago, IL, 2000)

Dalí, Salvador, *The Secret Life of Salvador Dalí*, trans. Haakon M. Chevalier (New York, 1942)

——, *The Unspeakable Confessions of Salvador Dalí, as Told to André Parinaud*, trans. Harold J. Salemson (New York, 1976)

Davis, Mary E., *Classic Chic: Music, Fashion, and Modernism* (Berkeley, CA, 2006)

De la Haye, Amy, and Shelley Tobin, 'The Dissemination of Design from Haute Couture to Fashionable Ready-to-Wear during the 1920s', *Textile History*, XXIV/1 (1993), pp. 39–48

——, *Chanel: The Couturière at Work* (Woodstock, NY, 1994)

Delay, Claude, *Chanel Solitaire*, trans. Barbara Bray (New York, 1974)

Déon, Michel, *Pages Françaises* (Paris, 1999)

Etherington-Smith, Meredith, *Patou* (New York, 1983)

——, *The Persistence of Memory: A Biography of Dalí* (New York, 1992)

Evans, Caroline, and Minna Thornton, 'Chanel: The New Woman as Dandy', *Women and Fashion: A New Look* (London, 1989), pp. 122–32

Fairchild, John, *Chic Savages* (New York, 1989)

Field, Leslie, *Bendor: The Golden Duke of Westminster* (London, 1983)

Flanner, Janet, *Paris was Yesterday, 1925–1939* (New York, 1972)

Font, Lourdes, 'L'Allure de Chanel: The Couturière as Literary Character', *Fashion Theory*, VIII/3 (2004), pp. 301–14

Galante, Pierre, *Mademoiselle Chanel*, trans. Eileen Geist and Jessie Wood (Chicago, IL, 1973)

Gere, Charlotte, *Marie Laurencin* (New York, 1977)

Gibson, Ian, *The Shameful Life of Salvador Dalí* (New York, 1997)

Gidel, Henry, *Coco Chanel* (Paris, 2000)

Gilbert, Martin, *Winston S. Churchill*, vol. V: *Companion Part I, 1922–1929* (London, 1979)

Gilbert, Sandra M., 'Costumes of the Mind: Transvestism as Metaphor in Modern Literature', *Critical Inquiry*, VII/2 (Winter 1980), pp. 391–417

Gold, Arthur, and Robert Fizdale, *Misia: The Life of Misia Sert* (New York, 1980)

Gronberg, Tag, 'Beware Beautiful Women: The 1920s Shopwindow Mannequin and a Physiognomy of Effacement', *Art History*, XX/3 (September 1997), pp. 375–96

Haedrich, Marcel, *Coco Chanel: Her Life, her Secrets*, trans. Charles Lam

Markmann (Boston, MA, 1972)

Hawes, Elizabeth, *Fashion is Spinach* (New York, 1938)

Helleu, Jacques, *Jacques Helleu and Chanel* (Paris, 2006)

Herald, Jacqueline, *Fashions of a Decade: The 1920s* (London, 1991)

Hill, Daniel Delis, *As Seen in Vogue: A Century of American Fashion in Advertising* (Lubbock, TX, 2004)

Holland, Ann, 'The Great Emancipator, Chanel', *Connoisseur* (February 1983), pp. 82–90

Horst, Horst P., *Salute to the Thirties* (New York, 1971)

Joseph, Charles M., *Stravinsky Inside Out* (New Haven, CT, 2001)

Kennett, Frances, *Coco: The Life and Loves of Gabrielle Chanel* (London, 1989)

Kirkland, Douglas, *Coco Chanel: Three Weeks* (New York, 2008)

Koda, Harold, et al., *Chanel* (New York, 2005)

Lawford, Valentine, *Horst: His Work and his World* (New York, 1984)

Leymarie, Jean, *Chanel* (New York, 1987)

Lifar, Serge, *Ma Vie: From Kiev to Kiev*, trans. James Holman Mason (New York, 1970)

Lipchitz, Jacques, *My Life in Sculpture* (New York, 1972)

Madsen, Axel, *Chanel: A Woman of her Own* (New York, 1990)

Mann, Carol, *Paris Between the Wars* (New York, 1996)

Mann, William J., *Kate, The Woman who was Hepburn* (New York, 2006)

Margetson, Stella, *The Long Party: High Society in the Twenties and Thirties* (Farnborough, Hampshire, 1974)

Margueritte, Victor, *La Garçonne*, trans. Hugh Barnaby (New York, 1923)

Marie, Grand Duchess of Russia, *A Princess in Exile* (New York, 1932)

Marny, Dominique, *Les Belles du Cocteau* (Paris, 1995)

Marquand, Lilou, *Chanel m'a dit* (Paris, 1990)

Morand, Paul, *Venices* [1971], trans. Euan Cameron (London, 2002)

——, 'On Proust and Chanel', trans. Vincent Giroud, *Yale Review*, XCIV/2 (April 2006), pp. 69–82

——, *The Allure of Chanel* [1976], trans. Euan Cameron (London, 2008)

Nabokov, Nicolas, 'Days with Diaghilev', *American Scholar*, XLIV/4 (Autumn 1975), pp. 620–35

New Yorker Magazine, *The New Yorker Book of War Pieces* (New York, 1947)

Peacock, John, *The 1920s (Fashion Sourcebooks)* (London, 1997)

Penn, Irving, and Diana Vreeland, *Inventive Paris Clothes, 1900–1939: A Photographic Essay* (London, 1977)

Phelps, Robert, ed., *Professional Secrets: An Autobiography of Jean Cocteau*, trans. Richard Howard (New York, 1970)

Picardie, Justine, *Coco Chanel: The Legend and the Life* (New York, 2010)

Picken, Mary Brooks, *Dressmakers of France* (New York, 1956)

Poiret, Paul, *King of Fashion: The Autobiography of Paul Poiret* [1931], trans. Stephen Haden Guest (London, 2009)

Polan, Brenda, and Roger Tredre, *The Great Fashion Designers* (Oxford, 2009)

Ponsonby, Loelia, *Grace and Favour: The Memoirs of Loelia, Duchess of Westminster* (New York, 1961)

Presley, Ann Beth, 'Fifty Years of Change: Societal Attitudes and Women's Fashions, 1900–1950', *The Historian*, LX/2 (1998), pp. 307–24

Rafferty, Jean Bond, 'Chanel No. 31', *France Today* (June 2009), pp. 30–32

Richards, Melissa, *Chanel: Key Collections* (London, 2000)

Ridley, George, with Frank Welsh, *Bend'Or, Duke of Westminster* (London, 1985)

Ries, Frank W. D., *The Dance Theatre of Jean Cocteau* (Ann Arbor, MI, 1986)

Roberts, Mary Louise, 'Samson and Delilah Revisited: The Politics of Women's Fashions in 1920s France', *American Historical Review*, XCVIII/3 (June 1993), pp. 657–84

——, *Civilization without Sexes: Reconstructing Gender in Postwar France, 1917–1927* (Chicago, IL, 1994)

Rowlands, Penelope, *A Dash of Daring: Carmel Snow and her Life in Fashion, Art, and Letters* (New York, 2005)

Russell, Rosalind, and Chris Chase, *Life is a Banquet* (New York, 1977)

Rzewuski, Alex-Ceslas, *La Double Tragédie de Misia Sert* (Paris, 2006)

Sachs, Maurice, *Witches' Sabbath* [1960], trans. Richard Howard (New York, 1964)

——, *The Decade of Illusion: Paris, 1918–1928*, trans. Gladys Matthews Sachs (New York, 1933)

Schiaparelli, Elsa, *Shocking Life* (New York, 1954)

Servadio, Gaia, *Luchino Visconti: A Biography* (New York, 1983)

Steele, Valerie, *Fashion and Eroticism: Ideals of Feminine Beauty from the Victorian Era to the Jazz Age* (Oxford, 1985)

——, *Paris Fashion: A Cultural History* (Oxford, 1988)

——, *Women of Fashion: Twentieth-Century Designers* (New York, 1991)

——, *Fetish: Fashion, Sex and Power* (Oxford, 1996)

Stewart, Mary Lynn, *For Health and Beauty: Physical Culture for Frenchwomen, 1880s–1930s* (Baltimore, MD, 2001)

—— with Nancy Janovicek, 'Slimming the Female Body? Re-evaluating Dress, Corsets, and Physical Culture in France, 1890s–1930s', *Fashion Theory*, V/2 (2001), pp. 173–94

Troy, Nancy J., *Modernism and the Decorative Arts in France* (New Haven, CT, 1991)

Veillon, Dominique, *Fashion Under the Occupation* [1990], trans. Miriam Kochan (New York 2002)

Vilmorin, Louise de, *Mémoires de Coco* (Paris, 1999)

Wallach, Janet, *Chanel: Her Style and her Life* (New York, 1998)

Walsh, Stephen, *Stravinsky: A Creative Spring: Russia and France, 1882–1934* (New York, 1999)

Wilson, Elizabeth, *Adorned in Dreams: Fashion and Modernity* (Berkeley, CA, 1987)

Wiser, William, *The Crazy Years: Paris in the Twenties* (New York, 1983)

——, *The Twilight Years: Paris in the Thirties* (New York, 2000)

Acknowledgements

My thanks to Dominique Nabokov for interview suggestions, and to Bettina Graziani and Claude Delay for talking with me about Chanel. I am grateful for the assistance of the staff at the Bibliothèque Nationale, the Bibliothèque Galliera of the Musée de la Mode, the library of the Musée des Arts Décoratifs and the Bibliothèque Historique in Paris; Karen Cannell at the library of the Fashion Institute of Technology and the librarians at the Billy Rose Theater Collection of the New York Public Library. Amy Syrell and the staff of the Scribner Library at Skidmore College assisted with countless requests for interlibrary loans, which were indispensable for my research. My thanks also to Skidmore College for a sabbatical semester in which to work on this book and funding to help with research costs. I am indebted to Thilo Ullmann, Mason Stokes, Sarah Goodwin, Sari Edelstein, Susannah Mintz and Margo Mensing for insights and encouragement. At Reaktion Books, Vivian Constantinopoulos has been enthusiastic from the start, and I am honoured to be working with her and her colleagues. My friends, family and many students – especially my Paris seminar class – have been waiting eagerly for this book. I hope they are pleased with it.

Photo Acknowledgements

The author and publishers wish to express their thanks to the following sources of illustrative material and/or permission to reproduce it:

© Photo Cecil Beaton: 110; © CHANEL: 77, 181, 184; © CHANEL – Collection Denise Tual: 12; © CHANEL/Courtesy VOGUE Paris: 70; © CHANEL – Photo Serge Lido: 142; © Comoedia Illustré 1910 Photo Félix/All rights reserved: 26; © Condé Nast/Corbis: 124; The Costume Institute, Metropolitan Museum of Art, New York, NY: 64 (Purchase Irene Lewisohn Bequest, 1975), 67 (Isabel Shults Fund, 1984), 92 (Purhase Various Funds, 1998), 116 (Rogers Fund, 1974), 158 (Gift of Bradford Dillman, 2004); © Dalmas/SIPA: 164; © R. Doisneau/Rapho: 155; © Peter Fink, ADAGP 2011: 153; Photo V. H. Grandpierre © All rights reserved/Courtesy of Vogue Paris: 118; Photo François Kollar © Ministère de la Culture – France: 111; © Lipnitzki/Roger-Viollet: 6; Photo Jean Moral © Brigitte Moral: 122; © Michael Ochs Archives: 15; © TopFoto/Roger-Viollet: 93; © All rights reserved: 25, 36–7, 41, 51, 54, 57, 86, 95, 156, 165.